BECAUSE OF BURT ...

by Mark Fauser

© 2019 Mark Fauser

All rights reserved. No part of this publication may be reproduced, stored in a retrieval system, or transmitted, in any form or by any means, electronic, mechanical, photocopying, recording, or otherwise, without the prior written permission of the author, except in the case of brief quotations embodied in critical reviews and certain other noncommercial uses permitted by copyright law.

For permission requests, write to the author, with subject "Permission Request," at the email address Mfauser@indy.rr.com.

ISBN: 0-9992125-3-2
ISBN-13: 978-0-9992125-3-0

This book is dedicated to Burt Reynolds and all of the great teachers who invest in kids to do their very best!

It's not easy for parents to see the highs and lows of your child so thank you, Mom and Dad, for teaching me discipline, love, and tenacity.

To my wife and kids … What a journey! I love you very much and want the best for you ALWAYS.

To all of my friends in St. Louis, Parkway Central High School, The University of Missouri, the Pikes, Jupiter Florida, Burt's Apprentices (The Avengers), New York, Los Angeles, Indiana and throughout the world who believed in me … thank you for being a part of my journey. You encouraged me and treated me the same whether I was up or down. That's friendship. Thank you to my teachers Jim Miller, Betty Pfaff, Mrs. Stivers, Weldon Durham, Richard Klepac, Larry Clark and of course Dom DeLuise, Charles Nelson Reilly, and Burt Reynolds who shared their knowledge and passion to me. To my students … who loves you? I do. Please pay it forward and make a difference! What a beautiful cover and back of the book by the amazing Dawn Darga, who helped me build CSA. A giant thanks to my best friend Rich Petrofsky, Mary Eckerle, Diana Gardner, Terry Lakes and of course Julie Fauser for giving me notes, and sifting through my awful grammar to make your read significantly better than it would have been without these remarkable people. Thank you, Jamy Bechler, for producing it into book form.

Who loves everybody? I do

BECAUSE OF BURT…
by Mark Fauser

On September 6th, 2018, I was preparing to do a show for our community outdoors in the beautiful Gardens Of Matter Park where my wife works. Suddenly, my phone started to blow up with messages, text's, Facebook beeps, with the tragic news that Burt Reynolds; my teacher, boss, mentor, and friend of over 32 years had just passed away.

Just as I started to lose it, as if Burt was right there, I could lovingly hear him say, "Hey putz! What the hell are you doing? I trained you better than that! The show must go on! We'll deal with this later." I was so comforted and almost chuckled out loud. I sensed him. Felt him. My training from Burt kicked in, and we did the show. The performances were great and coming to an end, and as if the tears from heaven couldn't hold it back anymore it started to pour down rain. The show was a success, and I went home, and then my tears began to pour.

Burt Reynolds was one of the most iconic film stars of all time, and yet to me, he was so much more. I knew how excited he was to work with Quentin Tarantino and that terrific cast the following month. How could this be? He had so much more to showcase as an artist.

That night I started to cathartically write stories about Burt and our times together on Facebook. Many of my friends suggested I should write a book to share these incredible stories about this legend. Thanks to all of them, I was inspired to honor the man who did so much for my family and me and take a crack at it.

Because of Burt, I was able to act and write for Academy Award winners, Tony Award winners, Emmy Award winners, and Grammy Award winners! Writing movies, TV shows and plays are one thing, because I could hide behind characters. Writing a book is a whole different beast. In 1986, at Burt's old dinner theater, we had a class with famed modeling agent, Nina Blanchard. Nina gave me an honest assessment of myself in front of the entire class. "Your nose is too big, and you have terrible grammar." In reading this book, you won't have to worry about my nose, but the grammar could be an issue at times … forgive me.

The stories are just too important not to share. Burt, you said, "We'll deal with this later." Well, later is now B-man. So, buckle up Smokey fans, as we go on this crazy ride with the Bandit …

Burt was loving on me with Charlie Durning to my right. I was so blessed to work with them.

- Because of Burt, I wanted to be a famous movie star!
- Because of Burt, I went to his school at the Burt Reynolds Dinner Theater and received an incredible education.
- Because of Burt, I received my Equity Card and did professional theater.
- Because of Burt, I met my wife and now have a beautiful family.
- Because of Burt, I learned to have a strong work ethic and have peers I love for a lifetime.
- Because of Burt, I was given the opportunity to serve as his personal assistant for two years.
- Because of Burt, I was hired to act on his show, and he helped me land another TV series.
- Because of Burt, I was hired to write for his TV show and other projects.
- Because of Burt, I met and worked with some of the biggest names in show business.
- Because of Burt, I had a front-row seat to stardom and became terrified of fame's price.
- Because of Burt, I wrote and acted in several studio movies.
- Because of Burt, I paid it forward and built a school for the arts in the Midwest.
- Because of Burt, I was blessed to have a teacher, boss, mentor, and friend for over 32 years.
- Because of Burt, I am compelled to share with you my incredible journey with one of the most legendary movie stars of all time and to give back to the man who gave me so much.

I am just one of many "Because of Burt" stories! I feel confident that Burt knew my love for him and sincere gratitude, but since his passing, I needed to recall my blessings and share them with the world. He was an extraordinary giver. Burt was loving, thoughtful, resilient, rugged, hot-tempered, complex, cocky, sensitive and that fun guy you saw on the big screen. He was that and so much more.

To me, it's important to give thanks to one of the most important people I've ever had in my life, and I want to do it Because of Burt …

With Burt in his home.

My goals for this book are:

1. To honor Burt Reynolds.

2. To tell of my journey and how it was massively influenced because of Burt Reynolds.

3. To share great Hollywood stories & anecdotes and to educate those readers who may choose to pursue the business and make their journey easier.

4. To have the world learn of Burt's tremendous, generous heart and see the value of paying it forward.

My passion for acting started when I was a kid and only grew after seeing Burt Reynolds on the big screen. That fun, classic laugh, and swagger are what I wanted to do Because of Burt …

... I WANTED TO BE A FAMOUS MOVIE STAR

Growing up in the '70s, Burt Reynolds was the biggest movie star on the planet. He was handsome, funny, robust, and self-effacing. The women loved him, and guys wanted to be like him. For five years in a row, Burt was the biggest box office star, and nobody had ever done that before or since.

When you went to the movies in the '70s, they were events. There weren't any Netflix, Blockbuster, DVD's, or videotapes to watch these movies again. If you missed one, you missed out and, with Burt Reynolds, you did not want to miss out.

Burt signed this picture from "Deliverance" and gave it to me.

As a young kid dreaming of being an actor, I saw various attributes in Burt's movies that I found intriguing. In *Deliverance,* he was a cocky tough guy in complete control until he hurt himself and had no power. Then, he had to depend on others for survival.

I saw him in *The Longest Yard* where he played a flawed character who used his leadership skills to pull out the best in others.

I laughed at him in *The End*, a dark comedy about a man who finds out he doesn't have much longer to live. He took a dark subject and found humor in it, heart and pathos. The movie showed the brilliance of Dom DeLuise and what a great reactor Burt Reynolds was to the insanity around him. Burt also directed the film, so he was starting to put his fingerprints both in front of and behind the camera.

Hooper was Burt paying homage to the people who sacrifice their bodies for others but never get the credit. It was Burt's love for the little guy.

Burt did many of his own stunts, and stuntmen and crew members loved him. Those stunts took a toll on him later in life, but I don't think Burt would have had it any other way.

In *Starting Over* Burt played entirely against type to show his range as an actor. He was in a triangle of great actors, two out of the three of whom were nominated for an Academy Award.

In *Sharky's Machine* Burt was a tough guy, played truthfully. When they cut off his fingers, he didn't play it like a "tough guy" and grimace; he instead, cried in agony … that was truthful. He also directed it.

Best Friends was funny, touching, and showed that sometimes you could love somebody, but it might not work out in that way you hoped.

Best Little Whorehouse in Texas showed there wasn't anything Burt couldn't do. He sang and surrounded himself with his incredibly talented friends in a movie that worked.

Because of Burt, we have gag reels. Before Burt, gag reels were used sporadically, but never to the magnitude and big stage that he put them on. The success of his gag reels is why you see them today on virtually every DVD and Blu-ray release. Think about it; back then film was used to make movies, and it was costly not only to shoot film but also to process and edit it. Therefore, if an actor messed up his or her lines, it was expensive, frowned upon and taboo. Not to Burt. He worked hard and played hard and knew people made mistakes. He had no problem showing those mistakes in what was labeled bloopers in *Cannonball Run* and *Smokey and the Bandit II*. It gave the audience an insight as to how much fun they had on the set. The success of the bloopers would help bring people back to pay to watch the movie again and again. So, whenever you watch gag reels or bloopers, please note: It's mostly Because of Burt.

Because of Burt, CB's became a huge thing. Before we had cell phones, the big fad, thanks to *Smokey and the Bandit* and Burt Reynolds was to have CB's from car to car.

When Burt was on the *Tonight Show* with Johnny Carson, it was another must-see TV. Bedtime would have to wait if Burt was on because something spectacular would happen to make us laugh.

When you watched an actor like Burt Reynolds that is handsome, funny, a badass, not afraid to play against type, poked fun at himself, surrounded himself with talented friends, had fun at what he did and made a lot of money … that is what I wanted to do for a living Because of Burt …

... BURT REYNOLDS DINNER THEATER

At the height of Burt Reynolds' career, the biggest movie star on the planet decided to give back to his community and build a dinner theater in Jupiter, Florida, which at the time, was just a small town. Burt created a safe place where professional actors could get away from the rat race of NY or LA and bring their talents to explore while also enjoying a beautiful paradise. The dinner theater would employ cooks, waiters, waitresses, box office attendants, development people, stage managers, set builders, costumers, musical directors, choreographers, directors, and actors. Stars like Sally Field, Carol Burnett, Dom DeLuise, Kirstie Alley, Farrah Fawcett, etc. would come to town and work for a month or so. Burt created and built an apprentice training program that would select a few actors for an entire year to give them the full education of the ups and downs of the business. While providing a priceless well-rounded education that the apprentices were paid to do for a hundred dollars a week. If you survived the year, in the end, you would get your Equity card – which is membership in a union that allows you to act on Broadway and in professional shows for a protected wage. In 1985, I auditioned to get into this program, and it would change my life forever …

Each year a few hundred people auditioned to get into the program. Each person who auditioned had to perform a comedic and dramatic monologue; sing a song in front of Charles Nelson Reilly and a panel of judges and perform a dance number taught by a choreographer. Overall, you had about five or ten minutes to shine. I was blessed to be selected as one of eleven actors and two stage managers in the class of 1986/1987.

Being selected into the Burt Reynolds Institute for Theater Training was a cross between the TV shows *American Idol* and *Survivor*.

It was like *American Idol*, because out of hundreds of people auditioning, they would only choose 10 to 15 people from around the country to make it, and many times we would have to perform at different venues, work together in shows and scenes and compete against each other for roles.

I say, *Survivor*, because we would get paid so little, it was not enough money to live. Working with each other often seven days a week for 12 to 15 hours, juggling a multitude of responsibilities it would often cause temporary factions or tensions that would want you to vote one of them off the island at any given time.

My year there started in January 1986. The first night at the theater, my fellow apprentices and I were in formal wear in Burt Reynolds personal box to watch the closing of *Man of La Mancha*. We were treated like stars, with a beautiful dinner served by a waitress, who was pretty, professional and who would later become the most important person in my life.

Our 1986 Burt Apprentice Class. From Left to right Front Row: Jack Esformes, Sandra Franck, Joanie Burton, Chris Lavely, Steve Ray. Back Row: Me, Roxanne Fay, Rudy Prieto, Montoya Allen, Jamie McMurray, Caroline Cornell, Merri Sugarman, Liz Snyder

My apprentice class was comprised of very talented people and lifelong friends. I remember after a great meal/show, and all of us dressed to kill, we went backstage to see some of the exhausted apprentices, actors, and stagehands who were relieved, but all kind of looking at us like … "do you have any idea what you are in for?" The next day we were all quickly humbled. We were asked to wear junk clothes as our job was to tear down the set. We all worked hard and took the set down. We were hot and sweaty, but then we had to drive it to the city dump and unload it. As we all stood out in the sweltering heat, with the immense stink of all of the garbage and the buzzards flying over us, I wondered if this was foreshadowing of my future.

What a stark contrast from the night before in suits and dresses eating a great meal with drinks on the house watching an equity show and now, we are at the bottom of the food chain with buzzards flying over us. That was part of Burt's design for us -to be prepared for the highs and lows of the business and to see if we could handle it.

Our first show was a play called *Orphans*. Directed by Leonard Frye, it starred Judd Nelson, the hugely popular actor from *The Breakfast Club*, Pat Hingle, the great character actor from *Hang Em High* with Clint Eastwood and a former apprentice and successful actor John D'Aquino who would later be a beloved lifelong friend of mine. With only three male roles in the first show, the guys had to read the script and audition for the director to see who would understudy who. In sports, I loved to compete against other people, and there were winners and losers, and I always wanted to

The Cast from *Orphans* Pat Hingle, Judd Nelson, John D'Aquino, and me.

win. In this business, it was/is my philosophy to compete against myself and not others. I couldn't control whether my looks were right, my height, my voice, etc.... So much of it was out of my control so you just have to do the best you could and let the chips fall where they may. Fortunately, I was right for the role I wanted and understudied John.

Our job was to know the stars lines, their blocking, to be ready to go on in an emergency in case. It was to become their personal assistant, take care of things they need whether it was to get them drinks, food, run lines with them or whatever, and then make sure you clean their dressing rooms and toilet after every performance. The rest of the apprentices would work some aspect of the show whether it was sound, lights, fly's, props, etc.

I was working nonstop and loving it. I was so blessed to be learning alongside Pat Hingle, an iconic character actor and Judd Nelson, a bona fide movie star!

However, perhaps the best thing is that I was able to learn from John D'Aquino, a former apprentice who had been there, done that and was working in Hollywood. John was patient and kind, and I loved his work ethic. He honestly remembered what it was like as an apprentice, and I couldn't have asked for a more comforting way to start the year off. The show was terrific, and everyone was great in it. Judd and I loved talking about sports and he, like Jack Esformes (my fellow apprentice), were big Boston fans. So, Judd was cool to me but had some oddities that I had never witnessed before. He was extremely superstitious. Once Judd was ready to enter the stage, it was like watching someone playing hopscotch trying to avoid cracks in the ground that he didn't want to step on or he had to go back to the starting point and do it again. He didn't want anyone around him when he was hopping over cracks either, or that too would cause him to go back, and he would get angry not knowing that if we didn't go to our places, we would get screamed at by someone else. He also didn't want anyone to talk to him once he was into his zone which was understandable to a degree, but nobody knew when he was in or not, so it was often problematic.

A veteran like Pat Hingle didn't pay any attention to it, and Judd knew that – John was not susceptible to it either except one time during intermission out of nowhere Judd came into the adjoining dressing room and was upset about something that happened on stage. John was calm but confused why this was going on in the middle of a show, but this altercation amped up quickly and the next thing you know I was in-between both of them breaking up a fight.

The next day I was called up to the Creative office to share what I witnessed, and I was honest and truthful. Again, I like Judd and think he is a terrific actor, but right is right and wrong is wrong and what I saw was just flat out wrong. The result was I was wrong! Right is not right and wrong can be right if you are the bigger star! It was a lesson I abhorred and refused to want to believe was true. I was shocked that John was admonished and Judd was unscathed. Where was the justice? I felt bad for John, I was outraged by the injustice, but I also felt terrible for Judd. He was a young guy, a talented guy, a good guy that I liked, but he needed to know wrong from right too, just like the rest of us and how was this going to help him long term? Is this what showbusiness does to people? It makes nobody's into somebody's, and when you reach a certain status you become right even if you are wrong? That's not fair to anyone. Sorry but to me that's wrong, but who was I? I am just an apprentice on my first show with a lot to learn.

January 26th, 1986 was the Superbowl between the Chicago Bears and Judd's favorite team, the New England Patriots. We had a matinee that day, and my understanding was that Judd wanted to watch the pre-game stuff, so we were going to be the first show ever to cancel at the Burt Reynolds Theater. What??? Did Burt Reynolds know this? Why couldn't my fellow apprentice Steve Ray go on for him? What will this do to my main man Burt (whom I haven't met yet)? What would this do to the reputation of the theater? What would this do to the waiters and waitresses who depend on that money? What happens to everyone who already bought tickets? Whatever happened to the show must go on? Why was this bothering me so bad? Why couldn't I shut my mouth and stay in my lane and say … "thank God I get the day off too and get to watch the Superbowl?"

Nobody knows what goes on in other people's personal life, but Judd's stardom rocketed to the top quick. That is the dream we all thought we wanted, but when dealing with it – there is no handbook on how to navigate and how potentially unhealthy and dangerous it can be.

Judd was young, and we were young. We all made many mistakes — too many. Only they were not in the high-profile spotlight like Judd's. We often blame the famous stars for misbehaving and that is easy for us to do, but we never look at the creator of the problem. Without Dr. Frankenstein, there is no Frankenstein, and we, as a society, are all a part of the creation of **MONSTERS**. Please note: I am not saying that Judd was a monster because he wasn't ... but Burt was giving us a glimpse of the extremes and dangers of stardom. To his credit, Judd Nelson has stood the test of time and is doing great, and I couldn't be happier for him.

John D'Aquino and I said goodbye to each other, and he gave me $100 tip for being his understudy, which was huge for me back then. It was a week's pay. He was a big brother to me, and I truly knew I gained a friend for life.

We were also doing a show called *House of Blue Leaves* for a short run that most of us starred in. My dear friend Jack Esformes didn't get cast in that either and was getting frustrated. My philosophy, right or wrong is that if you work hard, have talent, luck, faith and can weather the storm there is enough to go around for everybody to share the spotlight. Jack had the talent but could he weather the storm?

The next show was *Taken In Marriage* directed by actor Monte Markham. It starred Sachi Parker (Shirley MacLaine's daughter), Deborah Raffin, Betsy Palmer (from *Friday the 13th* fame) and Vera Miles, another huge star from the movie *Psycho*. I would love to go by Betsy Palmer and make the *Friday the 13th* sound effects and say "Kill her, mommy. Kill her." Betsy had a wicked sense of humor, and all of the ladies were great. One of the actresses (not mentioned above) was fired on final dress rehearsal night. Our apprentice team was called from the bullpen, and it was one of our own ... Roxanne Fay was asked to step up. Montoya, our stage manager, had called her early in the morning of final dress (the morning of opening night) and Montoya went through the show with Roxanne. Roxanne had to be ready to go with lines and blocking and had never rehearsed with the group of actresses before. Since there was not enough time for Roxanne to get costumed, she had to wear someone else's dress and had to borrow a bra from Vera Miles. All of the actresses and team members rallied around Roxanne. The pressure was immense, and Roxanne was out there representing all of us. Burt wanted us prepared for anything in life and when the coach called your name you better be ready to go and seize the **OPPORTUNITY**. Roxanne was not only ready, but she also killed it and was later nominated for a Carbonell Award, which is one of the highest honors in Florida.

Amongst the chaos of working mainstage shows, apprentice shows, there were various events that we had to do like television commercials for an Astrologer named Sandra. Prepping for the next play, coming to the theater, or do a runway show for clothes as a model, having scene work prepared in case any of the Master teachers showed up, and then one incredible, hysterical and brilliant teacher was coming to Jupiter Florida Because of Burt ...

... CHARLES NELSON REILLY

We were informed that Charles Nelson Reilly, our Master Teacher (oversaw all of our teachers), was coming to town and we should be ready. Charles was well known for being a regular on *Match Game,* the daily game show. I also remembered him from *Lidsville,* the Saturday kids show growing up on or the Bic Banana Commercial. His personality was bigger than life, and he was even funnier in person. He was affectionate and passionate about paying it forward from what he learned from his teacher Uta Hagen. He would plant seeds with us that the acting classes he took when he was our age were just filled with regular people like us ... Hal Holbrook, Jack Lemmon, Orson Bean, Robert Culp, Charles Grodin, Harvey Korman, Steve Mcqueen, Frank Langella, Geraldine Page, Ann Meara, and Jerry Stiller. Wow. What if that could be us someday?

With the Master ... Charles Nelson Reilly.

In addition to being hysterical, Charles was in the original Broadway production of *Bye Bye Birdie* with Dick Van Dyke. He won a Tony for his role in the Broadway Original production of *How To Succeed In Business Without Really Trying*, with my future next door neighbor Robert Morse. Charles was nominated for another Tony for the Broadway Original production of *Hello Dolly*. He was also nominated for a Tony as a director in *The Gin Game* where he directed Julie Harris who won a Tony for her performance in *The Belle of Amherst*. He also was nominated for 4 Emmy Awards. Bottom line, he was the real deal and sadly the perception of what he was, never matched the reality of what he was … a genius.

Some of the many lessons Charles would teach us were … the writer writes the black on the page, but the actor fills out all of the white on the page. Think of how brilliant that is?

Everyone will read the lines, but what an actor does between the lines will separate themselves from the others.

Another thing Charles was great at was putting a prop in the show. Give the prop a beginning, middle, and end, and people will remember it. It was amazing to watch him act while creating business with a prop …. There is nothing I could write that would ever do his brilliance justice.

Our Master Teacher worked with the biggest names in the business and passionately wanted us to do the **WORK** and make a difference … I can't tell you how comforting that was to all of us. My teammates brought their A-game to class, and all did very well.

That night we were invited to one of many of Burt's beach houses to celebrate. This is where Charles would stay when he came to town with the ocean in his backyard. No dinner theater food, but pasta and all the drinks we wanted. Wearing his comfortable nightgown, sipping on some Manhattan's, Charles made us scream with laughter, and helped us all feel like we belonged. Being from the Midwest, I was around gay people before but never someone who was so open and free about it. He was extremely comfortable in his skin, and his personality was magnetic.

He would kiss us affectionately like a loving parent and would poke fun at himself talking about how his mother would scream out the window when he picked up the baseball bat as a kid, and she would yell "hit the ball Mary"! Just as he talks with the high-pitched recognizable voice, he would break into a deep macho voice and jokingly introduce himself to us and shake our hands and say … "Chuck Reilly"! He told us about his father, a talented artist, who was asked to partner with a gentleman and go to Los Angeles. His mother screamed at his father that they were not leaving New York. But he said, "we would be equal partners to open this new company" and she put the squash to it and they stayed in their apartment. The gentleman and company he was referring to was … Walt Disney. Charles let's out a scream as if he would love to wring his mother's neck for that one. This story was not only interesting but had a profound effect on me.

If one gives you an opportunity in life – take it! Charles told us another story that on every Christmas Eve night at 12:00 am Eastern his mother for whatever reason would violently knock down the Christmas tree. Many years later after Charles was successful and in Los Angeles, he and his mother were driving in a pretty severe storm. Suddenly, a massive Christmas tree near the Playboy Mansion crashed down right in front of their car. Charles calmly looked at his watch and said, "It's 9:00 pm mother which means it's 12:00 am in New York. Right on cue."

The thing I found so funny, yet so heart-warming about Charles is that many of his stories and a lot of his comedy is derived from great pain as it is for most comedic actors. He lived through the worst years of being gay – he was teased, even by his own mother, but Charles never pretended to be anything but who he was. I have so much love and respect for him. Charles was tremendously confident and yet extremely insecure like most of us pained actors. Charles would share with us his insecurities … so we didn't feel abnormal for feeling the way we would at times. He told me he had a panic attack before the Broadway opening of *How To Succeed in Business Without Really Trying* and said to the director he couldn't do it. They were days away from opening, and Charles was frozen in fear. "Don't do it for you. Do it for me." Instructed the director.

Something about that clicked to Charles and me. "We perform for others! We sacrifice, cry, laugh, starve for the love of our art … but we do it for them." Charles went on to do that Broadway show and won a Tony Award.

His stories were fascinating and his teaching even better. This was a great first day and night with him. There would be many more to come, but we had to go home and get ready for class, work and various other jobs the following day. Charles knew everyone in the business but was adamant to us – it's about the **WORK**. Study. Study. Study! Work on your craft and if it is meant to be the rest will come. On behalf of all of my fellow apprentices before and after us … here is a toast to the great Charles Nelson Reilly.

An incredible teacher, director, mentor, and friend, Charles became a considerable part of my life and so many other people's lives. The Master Teacher, the classes, the parties and stories with Tony Award-winning Charles Nelson Reilly were only possible Because of Burt …

... BACK TO B.R.I.T.

B.R.I.T. stood for Burt Reynolds Institute for Theater Training. Our next show was *A My Name Is Alice* starring the powerhouse singer Marilyn McCoo from the 5th Dimension.

From the movie, *Saturday Night Fever* was the personable Donna Pescow. I could imitate John Travolta to a tee, so don't think I didn't have fun interacting with Donna throughout our time there.

Merri Sugarman, my fellow classmate, was not only understudying the iconic Marilyn McCoo but was star struck like the rest of us.

This story is best told by Merri...

"Marilyn was offered a Pepsi commercial that was to shoot in Atlanta during the run.

With Marilyn McCoo

One night during the show I got a message to come up to the office – I had a phone call. Of course, I was sure someone had died. I picked up the phone, and this is what I get.

Merri, it's Burt. I want to let Marilyn go do this Pepsi commercial. It's for the 2 billionth anniversary or some sh*t, and she should get to be in it. I'm told you're not only ready, but you're good. You okay to do this?

Seriously?!?!? Whoever the F said I was ready was a liar because all I had was a notebook with a lot of blocking written down. I went on. Both my parents were there. They had recently split up, and this was the first time they'd breathed the same air since. I was a mess. I finished the opening, and I fell from a moving platform in the blackout before a quick change that was literally about 15 seconds long. It was only the 10' high platform the band was on.

As I fell, I pulled down all the speaker wire grasping for anything – and hit the stage on my knees just as the other platform came in. That platform was only a few inches high, and I hit it bent at the waist. I broke all my ribs, but I didn't know it. I finished the show on pure adrenaline. Burt had a little surprise. Congrats party all set up in the lobby after the show.

At the end of it, my parents took me to the emergency room. Burt sent 2 dozen roses the next morning with a card that read "You are what the Institute is about."

That card is in Merri's wallet to this day because and she says "sometimes we all need reminding that someone saw us do something they thought was extraordinary right? You make one person feel that way in your life, and you are the extraordinary one." That was Burt Reynolds! Merri goes on to say, "You make as many people feel that way as Burt did in his lifetime and you should be able to rest easy about what's coming next when you pass."

What an education we all had. Two of our apprentices were called on to deliver under impossible pressure situations and did so with flying colors. We were not even a quarter of the way through and what an education. What an experience.

Saturday Night Fever with Donna Pescow.

One day we were called out to Burt's ranch which was massive to meet his parents and see Burt's horses and gift shop. He had a sleek black helicopter there too that could either stay on the ranch or fly to Burt's helicopter pad at his house. We discovered that Burt owned condo's, buildings, several beach houses in addition to his, restaurants, I mean, this guy owned the town.

Ten Little Indians was a show our apprentices did next, followed by our next Main Stage show which was *Little Shop of Horrors*. Again, I was lucky to get to understudy the role I wanted as the psychotic Dentist, but things were not great for the team overall.

Merri was injured with broken ribs. Another one of our actors became really sick and needed to leave the program for at least a month and on top of that my very talented compadre, Jack Esformes confided in me that he was thinking about calling it quits because he hadn't landed a part and wondered if it was in the cards.

Jack wanted off the island of Survivor, and I begged him not to quit.

One, he was a great friend, and I didn't want him to leave. Two, remember my philosophy, right or wrong, is that if you work hard, have faith, talent, and luck and you can weather the storm there is enough to go around for everybody to share the spotlight. He had the talent he just needed to keep the **FAITH** and weather the storm. Three, who the hell was going to help me move these fricken piano's up and down the stairs without two of our teammates already unavailable? With two people down, it made the workload harder for the rest. A month later, we were all exhausted and worn out. That's just how Burt Reynolds liked it and guess who was coming to town? The Man himself! Burt Reynolds.

... MEETING BURT REYNOLDS

We received notice that Burt Reynolds was in town and wanted us at his house that night because he wanted to teach a class. What??! We're going over to Burt Reynolds house?!!!! The man? The Legend? His home?!! Holy crap. This guy was my idol! We all knew we were going to meet him at some point, but it was go time.

On the way to Burt's house, which he called Valhalla, we were all in a van running our lines with our partners from scenes we had and were trying to stay focused. Everyone was talking over each other. It's like a bunch of crazy people all talking to themselves at once. Adrenaline was flowing as we pulled up to his gate and were buzzed in. We were going to see the Great OZ.

We traveled through a long winding driveway surrounded by gates and thick brush on each side. We saw a large house and were let out. "This is Burt's house?" I said. Our coach, Tom Sommerville says "No this is just his office. His house is up there"! Whoa! It was a complex.

Anxiously, we waited for the legend to show. Burt's office was filled with a massive library of books, his large game room filled with iconic memorabilia, awards, and pictures of Burt with stars throughout.

Suddenly, Burt Reynolds walked in. The guy I idolized from the big screen was now right in front of me in person, as handsome and charismatic as you see in the movies. He was very kind and shook everyone's hands. I looked at him all goo-goo eyed. My peers comfortably engaged with him, but I went from the usually cocky guy to a stuttering, mumbling monkey boy, and completely tongue-tied. I couldn't speak. I was staring at him like a stalker.

Mr. Reynolds was amazing and taught us things that were utterly foreign to us as stage actors. He shared with us the importance of the camera and the people working behind the camera. He taught us not to act but to "be" because the camera doesn't lie and will know you are acting. It catches the nuances and knows whether you are truthful or not.

He told us how legendary actor Lee Marvin, would always talk to the camera before each day of shooting because that relationship between the camera and actor is crucial to translate onto the big screen.

Burt would call up two of us to do scenes and every time we moved and then stopped, Burt would lay down a mark on the floor where we stopped. By the time the scene was over, you would see the various marks on the floor. The first mark, the second mark, the third mark, etc.... your marks and their marks. Burt told us when we do the scene again if we don't hit the marks precisely like we did the first time we would be out of focus because there's a camera operator, a focus puller, a camera assistant, director of photography and lighting designer who all depend on you hitting your marks.

Burt was our coach and teacher! The man who started it all.

Try memorizing your lines while "being" and not acting and knowing when you move and where your mark always is. It's not easy.

Then Burt added the props back to the original scene and said in the master shot when we saw everyone in the scene which hand did you have the cup of coffee? On what line did you drink it? How much did you drink? What line did you take your glasses off? What line did you put them back on your face?

He said, if you don't match the master shot on your other shots it won't match, and you'll compromise your director and editor's choices. What an overwhelming lesson to learn. You have to hit your marks, know what line you drank, know how much you drank, when you took your glasses off and when you put them back on and whatever you do don't ACT just BE. Be honest!!! Your art demands that you are honest!

He told a story about when Jack Nicholson did *One Flew Over The Cuckoo's Nest*. Mr. Nicholson did the scene with his usual brilliance and the crew laid down his marks. Once that is set the actor can go away while a stand-in is used in the actor's place so the crew can light, focus and simulate what the actor just did to get the shot to look beautiful. While Mr. Nicholson was away, the director of photography noticed a pillar was in his way to get the lighting the way he wanted. They were stuck; it just wouldn't look good. The director, Milos Forman, told Jack the problem with the lights and asked Jack if he wouldn't mind taking an extra two steps on that one cross. Jack kindly walked through it to see. He did the scene again, and it didn't feel natural. He tried again, and it just wasn't real. He really wanted to help, so he tried again, and he just couldn't do it without feeling fake and compromised.

He finally apologized, and without question, the construction crew started to make structural changes to the set to remove a structural support beam and have it braced in another place out of view to keep the integrity of the art real.

As if that wasn't enough info for me to try to process for one night, Burt went on to try to teach us and protect us from actor tricks. How some star actors will do the master shot with you. Then you do their close up, but when it's your turn for your close up … the arrogant star might not feel like doing it with you, so you have to act with a script supervisor or someone who is not an actor. You have to reach the same intensity or same emotion you did for the master and the star's close up but now this is your close up, and the person is reading the lines to you in a monotone fashion because they are not actors. That was tough and kind of gross. He said most actors are great people, but some could be jerks, and he just wanted to have us prepared and protect us.

Another thing Burt taught us was about not overlapping in dialogue in close-ups. He said it's great when you are doing the master shot of all of you, but you can't in close-ups because the sound won't match the master if you want to go back to it in the editing … so keep the close-ups clean and don't overlap.

He taught us a story about one of his first television series called *Riverboat* with Darren McGavin, best known for his roles in *A Christmas Story* and *The Night Stalker*.

Burt said, Darren would do the master shot and his close up, but sometimes if he didn't want the camera on the other actor for their closeup he would subtly hum throughout the take.

It was somewhat hard to detect while doing the scene, but in post, it was a nightmare to deal with and would pretty well assure they would not use the other actor's close up often because of the nagging humming sound. He told us to defend ourselves. Whether people value you or not, make your own dignity.

Here I am scrubbing a star's toilet.

Perhaps the most important lesson he taught us is that **EVERYBODY MATTERS**. Value everybody! Be a good person! "You do that because it's the right thing to do. Period." The crew, the production assistant, the secretary, the waiter, and busboy. The elderly, the handicapped, the kids! Color, gender, religion, sexuality, rich or poor everyone matters. You never know who is who and who is related to whom. You never know, who will help you because you were polite to them and believed in them, but again do it merely because it's the right thing to do.

Your audition started in the car, being kind to the parking attendant, to people in the elevator, in the casting office, and all the way home.

Sometimes, it seemed so surreal, here was this legendary movie star working with our apprentices calling them by name.

Burt did a thing I call the infamous "Burt Love Clutch." That's when he wraps his hands around your neck in a loving, intimate way to quietly advise, critique, and encourage into your ear to not publicly call you out, but to gently get you to know he loves you but push harder. Like a loving coach to their quarterback.

When he and Charles would do scene work, they would sometimes get excited and do the scene over and over again making tweaks here and there while working with the actors.

Burt would do the "Burt Love Clutch" whispering incredible words of encouragement. Sometimes they would watch the scene and say, "That was good. Real good. Next scene."

That happened to me. I was selfishly like, what the heck? I want the "Burt Love Clutch." Lovingly tell me how bad I sucked, just so I can get the "Burt Love Clutch" and this gigantic movie star says my name. In retrospect, you think I would be jumping up and down for joy that he said "That was good. Real good." but for some reason, I wanted more attention from him. Now I am competing with my peers. I am a total hypocrite and losing faith. I'm tired and struggling to weather the storm. What a terrible leader and friend I am. The next day we were back to cleaning toilets which were designed for us to get ready for the highs and lows of the business and I was surprisingly low.

We had another class with Burt, and he was saying everyone's name but mine, and I was his biggest fan of the group. What the hell!!!! Say my name Dammit! M-A-R- …. K! SAY IT! Burt was going to be leaving the next day to work with Liza Minelli on a movie – "Oh God please say my name before you leave." Nope! Dammit!!!! Later, I showed my mom a picture of Burt teaching our class and told her I wish he knew my name. She said based on the picture she thought I looked like I cared too much and that's probably why he didn't know my name. Really?!!! So, I should have gone to class and looked like I didn't care and then maybe he would say my name? Great, advise mom. Thanks. I'm not going to do that!

You know what … I'm acting like an immature baby! Just shut up and do what Charles Nelson Reilly advised … "Do the **WORK**." "Focus on the **WORK**."

We were now at about the halfway point of the year, and if my buddy Jack didn't land a role soon, he may leave the program. His luck was about to change in a big way, and I was about to meet the funniest person I ever met in my life, a person who would have a profound effect on my family and me. This all was possible Because of Burt …

... DOM DELUISE

With my lovable friend Dom DeLuise

The funniest person I ever met in my life ... Dom DeLuise came to town and stayed with us for over a month to direct *Brighton Beach Memoirs*. He brought his three talented sons: Peter, a brilliant director today and former star of *21 Jump Street*, Michael DeLuise, who is one of my dearest friends and a brilliant actor who starred in *Wayne's World* and *The Gilmore Girls;* and David DeLuise who would later star in *Wizards of Waverly's Place*.

Norman Fell, from *Three's Company,* was one of the stars of the show with a great cast and guess who landed the lead role? One of the best roles of the year? Yup! Our fellow apprentice Jack Esformes. We were all thrilled for him, and he was perfect for the part.

It was life-affirming to me that my motto was correct: If you work hard, have talent, luck and **FAITH** and weather the storm there is enough to go around for everybody to share the spotlight. Jack was on cloud nine, and he should have been. Joanie Burton another apprentice also landed a Main Stage show and played his sister. So cool! Being directed by Dom DeLuise and having this fantastic cast surrounding you was a dream come true.

I was Peter's understudy and really liked him a lot. Every day I would always sit next to Dom in rehearsals to learn as much from him as possible. Watching Dom direct was a show in and of itself. He would be constructing a prop in the middle of a scene and would appear to be disengaged from the actors performing, and once in a while I would notice Norman Fell looking at Dom as if to say, "Are you seeing what we are doing?"

And out of nowhere Dom would look at Norman and say, "What's your name?" Norman would look at him as if to say are you serious? Then Norman would say, "Norman?"

Dom "Yes! That's it! Good! Norman, walk over there when she's talking to you and lay down your suitcase." All of a sudden Dom would get frustrated with the prop he was working on and throw it down on the ground and scream in a deep voice, "Your mother's ass!"

I would laugh uncontrollably because it was a three-ring circus. Dom knew precisely what he was doing, but his tangents and his seemingly preoccupied manner may have had others thinking otherwise. Because of Dom's weight he would often fall asleep in the middle of rehearsals and asked me to nudge him if that was the case, but here was the fantastic thing ... The actors would be running their scenes and Dom would start to snore, and out of nowhere Dom would pop out of his seat and say, "Remember on that line go over to the pot and smell the cabbage." Everyone was in awe. Was Dom some kind of savant? How could Dom possibly know what just happened? His eyes were closed, and he was snoring. Literally snoring and yet he was completely aware and in control in his own entertaining, unique way.

Props, costumes, it didn't matter Dom's attention to detail was on another level. Very much like Charles. He insisted that the oven worked on stage because he wanted the smell of cabbage to permeate throughout the theater.

One of the things I noticed going into the opening is that not everyone or everything was ready. Jack was excellent and more than prepared, same with Joanie, but some didn't know their lines yet. Individual set pieces weren't complete, and most people would start to panic but not Dom.
He was calm, funny, made light of things, often fell asleep and snored and then popped up utterly aware of what just happened and scream out things that were brilliant. It was organized chaos but sitting next to him on the sideline, I began to question whether Dom knew the danger we were in.

What I learned was that he was in complete control. He had a lot more experience than I did, and panicking was not going to solve anything. He was calm and instilled **FAITH** to everyone that we would get there. The show opened, and sure enough, it was terrific.

What a great experience. It was so rewarding to see my buddy Jack Esformes, our fellow apprentice, and Joanie hit it out of the park. It was not only a massive victory for Jack but for all of us. That's how it worked. Jack was not going anywhere now except enjoying the accolades he richly deserved. To see where Jack was in his mind and spirit and to see where he ended up was very rewarding for my peers and me. Every laugh he received, every standing ovation for him at the curtain calls were just awesome.

Dom DeLuise and the DeLuise family were as genuine and kind as they get, and I felt so lucky to have had that month with them and prayed it was just the beginning of my relationship with the DeLuise Family. There would be other stellar talent showing up to educate and inspire us Because of Burt ...

... JASTON WILLIAMS

Jaston Williams, the writer, and star of *Greater Tuna* was coming to town to direct us in an original piece of monologues called *American Window*. Jaston was doing precisely what I wanted to do. He was writing and starring in his own work and somewhat in control of his own destiny. Don't wait for a casting director or someone else to figure out what you can do – show them what you can do with your own words. While Jaston was directing us, my friend and partner Brent Briscoe was touring the country with another great actor John Hawkes, who would be later nominated for an Academy Award, was doing *Greater Tuna* for Jaston and Joe Sears. Jaston was a loving, great director and really looked out for all of us.

Burt's apprentices were happy to have Jaston Williams with us. He is sitting on the couch furthest to the right.

The piece he had me do was something I really didn't want to do because I didn't think I could do it justice, but Jaston insisted and believed in me that I could deliver. It was a guy who was climbing the Continental Divide and deciding whether he should have a baby or abort it. It was well written, and I am glad he pushed me to do it, and it worked.

With Liz & Roxanne in *Big El's Best Friend*. My character was an Elvis wannabe.

He would come back months later and direct two one acts. One was *Baby With The Bath Water*, and the other was one of my favorite experiences *Big El's Best Friend*. I played a wackjob Elvis impersonator who was hired to help a crazed fan. As the show played out, we discovered that my character was sicker than the crazed fan with the addiction to Elvis. It was funny as hell, dark and pathetic. Shows the dark side of fame which I love and had a 3-person cast with terrific actresses and I loved it.

Jaston really cared for all of us, and he was so inspiring to me. Jaston makes an impact on others and pays it forward. My love and respect for him are through the roof. He had a significant influence on my life, and I will always be indebted to him for that.

There was a play called *Alone Again* which did three things for me. First, it gave me a break that I badly needed from learning lines and doing so much. Secondly, I learned from watching that play that my parents had a life too. It wasn't just all about us as kids, but they too deserved time to have fun and live after their many years of sacrifice. It's odd that it took this play or a piece of art for me to understand that. Finally, I met Tommy Thompson in the sound booth – who has a fantastic story that I must divert to Because of Burt …

... EVERYBODY MATTERS

Burt taught us that! **EVERYBODY MATTERS.** A pure ideology that is so often ignored, but, if applied would make the world such a better place. Tommy Thompson was/is a handsome guy, who had been paralyzed from the waist down due to a terrible car accident. Burt believed in Tommy and wanted to encourage him to keep fighting. Burt told him if he can get up to that sound booth every night, he would hire Tommy to be his sound man. So, every night, every show, Tommy, with crutches around each arm would struggle to get into the sound booth and operate the sound for the show. The struggle was so worth it. It gave him fight to have a mission in life, and once that was conquered, Burt would see how he could help you achieve your next purpose. Tommy would share with me his passion for writing. I loved his creativity. Supporting people's dreams is important. Tommy's story is remarkable, and when you read about what else he accomplished Because of Burt, you will be astonished. Tommy has a whole Because of Burt story too as do so many people.

Another example of Burt's compassion ... Jimmy Lewis was an apprentice, too, who had trauma from serving in the war. Burt appreciated his service to our country and hired Jimmy all of the time in a variety of fields. Scott Jackson, a former waiter, and bartender at the dinner theater became Burt's Executive Assistant for many years. Rob Kairalla, a former bartender at the dinner theater, became Burt's real estate agent and negotiated the deal of the dinner theater, his house, and other properties. Andy Kato was a waiter, and today Andy successfully runs the Maltz theater with great respect and honor to Burt.

Burt was relentless in his efforts to help others. One time he saw a street artist who was clearly struggling, but Burt loved the person's artwork. Burt told the artist to shower, clean up and bring his artwork to his house over the weekend. The struggling artist would show up dazed and confused and there at Burt's home would be Frank Sinatra, Dean Martin, Sammy Davis Jr., and a multitude of wealthy people for an impromptu auction. Within a few hours, the struggling artist went from barely feeding himself to a millionaire overnight and changed that person's life forever. This happened more than once with visual artists because of Burt.

Production assistants were watched over by Burt. If someone disrespected them, it didn't matter if you were a Studio Executive, you were going to have to deal with Burt. Apprentices were just that apprentices ... but to Burt, they were his kids. If you messed with them, Burt was going to open up a can of whoop ass.

Because of Burt .... Everyone matters. There was a lady named Sally Wagner who was in a wheelchair who lived near the theater. She was sweet and loved the theater and would want to hang out, but many times because of our work schedule we had to keep going ... but it was clear to everyone there that she was the first lady of the theater. If anyone disrespected, her Burt would get rid of you. It's an easy concept to just be kind and courteous to people. To try to find the best in people and go into everything you do knowing **EVERYBODY MATTERS**.

We had more lessons to learn and more work to be done Because of Burt ...

... THE REST OF THE YEAR

Here are some of the other shows we either performed in, understudied, or worked the crew for *Jacques Brel, Dancin', You're a Good Man, Charlie Brown, Getting My Act Together And Taking It On the Road,* and *We Don't Need No Stinking Badges*. We still had scene work, clean up, other

Mel Tillis in the center front with our class and some of our administrators.

shows to do and were plenty busy. In between all of the work, we would sometimes get a visit from stars: Liza Minelli and Regis Philbin, Ricardo Montalban, Carol Burnett, etc....

We did a musical called *Working*, an excellent show for a group of actors to do. The director had talent, but for some reason was insecure and questioning everything. We literally didn't know what was in the show or not until moments before the show started. Seriously, we had the ushers closing the door and not allowing the customers into the theater because we were rehearsing right up to the moment.

The huge lesson here for me was that some shows with the best director and the best laid out plans sometimes doesn't work for whatever reason. Sometimes the show that gets thrown together works out better because of the people around the project rally. I had a great team that was not going to let us fail.

The other thing I learned is that people in the entertainment industry who are creating something for the first time must have incredible **FAITH!** Whether people relate to God and faith is up to them. I'm just here to tell you ... this field is not 1 plus 1 equals 2. Creating something from scratch has no proven track record. What if it is not received as well as it was conceived?

Watching Dom, Charles, my teachers in college the people with experience have faith that it will all work out was great for me to observe, because, along the way, people around you doubt ... I did as well ... unless you have **FAITH** that it will all work out and keep battling, one will consider quitting due to the embarrassment of being on stage being ridiculed, booed or given bad reviews.

Charles Nelson Reilly came in to direct our last three shows. *Zelda* was a one-woman show where we were voices supporting Academy Award-nominated actress Piper Laurie.

Signing my first Equity Contract.

Our Equity Show was going to be *Annie*, with the brilliant Charles Nelson Reilly directing. What a credit. Our paycheck was now significantly more because we signed our equity contract. The catch-22 that Burt was so great at helping people overcome. You can't be in a professional stage show without being in Equity, and you can't be in Equity without doing a professional stage show. Because of Burt ... we were now all Equity.

I've been paid in Summer Repertory for acting on stage before but being an Equity actor, I would get paid more in one week than I would for the entire summer in rep.

Again, this was Burt's way of rewarding hard **WORK** and giving so much to others who were starting off in their careers. Burt was one of a kind, and this was just the tip of the iceberg that was his giving heart.

We worked in the day near the backstage restaurant for *Annie*, and at night we worked on another production at the theater for a paid audience which was the norm. In addition to us making good money now, we were going to end our year with the incredible talents of Alice Ghostley to play Miss Hannigan. Robert Fitch was the original Rooster on Broadway and came to Jupiter to do it with us, and Elliott Reid as President Roosevelt. Our Annie was a spectacular young actress named Lindsey Alley. The show was outstanding, and most of us played multiple roles. One of my roles was Lt. Ward interacting with Annie below.

DIAMOND HEAD (Lē'ahi) STATE MONUMENT

Honolulu, O'ahu

HISTORIC TRAIL TO THE SUMMIT

The trail to the summit of Lē'ahi was built in 1908 as part of the U.S. Army Coastal Artillery defense system. Entering the crater from Fort Ruger, through the Kapahulu Tunnel, the trail scaled the steep interior western slopes of the crater to the summit. The dirt trail with numerous switchbacks was designed for mule and foot traffic. The mules hauled materials on this trail for the construction of Fire Control Station Diamond Head located at the summit. Other materials were hoisted from the crater floor by a winch and cable to a midway point along the trail. The Kahala Tunnel was built in the 1940s and is the public entrance today.

HIKING THE TRAIL

From the trailhead to the summit of Diamond Head Crater, you will hike 0.8 mile (1.3 km) one way and climb 560 feet (171 m) from the crater floor. The trail follows an uneven and steep terrain requiring caution and appropriate footwear. Portions of the trail involve steep stairways - take your time. Other portions of the trail go through a long tunnel which is lighted. Allow 1.5 to 2 hours for a safe and leisurely round-trip hike.

After exiting the tunnel, turn right and take the 99 steps into the Fire Control Station up to the summit. To avoid congestion, take the loop trail along the rim and interior slope back to the tunnel.

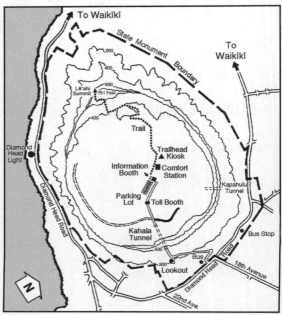

POINTS OF INTEREST ON THE TRAIL

1 The elevation at the trailhead on the crater floor is about 200 feet (61 m).

2 The former pistol ranges consist of earthen berms that are visible from the concrete path.

3 The trail conforms to the 1908 alignment with switchbacks up the steep interior slope.

4 Concrete Landing/Lookout. This concrete foundation held a winch and cable to lift materials from the crater floor to this point.

5 Steep stairway of 74 concrete steps leads into the first narrow tunnel.

6 Tunnel is lighted and 225 feet long.

7 Second stairway consisting of 99 steep steps with overhead beams to place camouflaging.

8 At the top of the stairs is the entry to the lowest level of the Fire Control Station with observation equipment for Fort DeRussy at Waikīkī.

9 The lighted spiral staircase accessed the 4 levels of the Fire Control Station. Go up the 52 stairs to the third level where the mounts for the observation equipment are still present.

10 Exit to the exterior of the crater through slits once covered with metal shutters. Note the rock and concrete that camouflage the outside.

11 The 54 metal stairs were installed in the 1970s and replaced the ladder to the summit.

12 The elevation of the crater summit and the uppermost level of the Fire Control Station is 761 feet (232 m).

13 From the summit, follow the trail along the rim and take the 82 metal steps down to the lower trail. This trail loops back to the tunnel.

14 Bunkers along the crater rim were built in 1915. Area closed - emergency helicopter landing.

15 Lookout provides sweeping views of southeastern O'ahu coastline towards Koko Head and the offshore islands of Moloka'i, Lana'i and Maui.

16 Rest stop offers views of the crater before heading back down through the tunnel.

HOW THE CRATER WAS FORMED

The pronounced seaward summit, deeply eroded ridges, and ovoid-shaped crater are evidence of Lēʻahi's very dynamic geological history. The creation of Oʻahu began around 2.5 to 4 million years ago with volcanic eruptions from 2 shield volcanoes. A period of extensive erosion followed, leaving the Koʻolau and Waiʻanae Mountain Ranges as the remnants of these volcanoes.

After about 1.3 million years of volcanic inactivity, the southeastern end of the Koʻolau Range erupted. These eruptions occurred under the ocean, where the magma was broken down into ash and fine particles by the water and steam. Blown into the air, these particles were cemented together into a rock called tuff which created tuff cones, such as Lēʻahi.

Lēʻahi is believed to have been formed about 300,000 years ago during a single, brief eruption. The broad crater covers 350 acres with its width being greater than its height. The southwestern rim is highest because winds were blowing ash in this direction during the eruption. Since the eruption, the slopes of the crater have been eroded and weathered by rain, wind, and the pounding of the sea. A coral reef now protects the seaward slopes of the crater.

Today, Lēʻahi (Diamond Head) is the most recognized landmark in Hawaiʻi. It was designated a National Natural Landmark in 1968 as an excellent example of a tuff cone.

ENVIRONMENT

The semi-arid climate, the steep rocky slopes, and the shallow soil of Diamond Head support mostly low shrubs and herbs. Botanists believe that the crater was once covered by a dryland forest, but only a few native Hawaiian species, such as *ʻilima*, remain.

ʻilima

Rainwater collects on the crater floor in the winter, creating a small lake that was frequented by native ducks and waterbirds until the early 1900s.

Most of the plants and animals you see in the crater today were introduced to Hawaiʻi after the 1800s. Dominant plants are the *kiawe*, a relative of the mesquite, and *koa haole*. Both of these plants were brought in as cattle feed and have adapted well to the hot, dry conditions. You may see some of the common introduced birds, such as cardinals, doves, and sparrows.

With Lindsey Alley as Annie who later became a Mouseketeer for Disney with Justin Timberlake, Brittany Spears, Christina Aguilera, and Ryan Gosling.

Another one of my roles was Howe, the assistant to the President. FDR was in a wheelchair, so I wheeled him around. Elliott was up there in age and would often forget his lines. He asked me to gently nudge him if he forgot his line and of course, I was happy to help.

One day during rehearsal, Elliot forgot his line, and per his instruction, I gave him a gentle nudge. In front of everyone, he screamed at me, "Stop it! Don't touch me! I know my line"! Charles looked over his glasses like what just happened. I was embarrassed that he would make a production of what he asked me to do to help him, but I also remember the lesson Burt taught us. Make your own **DIGNITY!**

Don't succumb to actor games. Protect yourself. So from that point on it was on … he was going to have to fend for himself. It wasn't long after that where he was exposed. During a party sequence, I was to wheel him out in his wheelchair where he was to say, "Merry Christmas!" I realized he wasn't paying attention and sitting next to Charles. So during my cue in rehearsal, I came on to stage with an empty wheelchair. There was silence. More silence. Then Charles turned to Elliott who was sitting next to him and said, "Aren't you forgetting something?" Everyone laughed, and the tables were turned. I was always respectful to Elliott, and the team bailed him out of problems virtually every night, including one night where he accidentally kicked over the American flag, and it hit the ground, and he said: "Burn that flag!"

Charles was a great director and teacher.

All in all, it was a great experience, and we knew our time was coming to an end there. We had one more swan song show to do, and it was time for us to leave the nest. The last show was a showcase, if you will where we could write our own stuff or do scenes and songs to create a final showcase for the audience, Burt, Charles, Loni, and others.

I wrote a Star Trek skit spoofing that the crew meant to beam down to Jupiter and wound up in Jupiter, Florida, and mocked the dinner theater food and the harsh conditions of work. We could hear Burt's classic laugh from his box. He was laughing hard and even though he didn't say my name ever ... I could tell that he loved that skit from his iconic laugh. Merri Sugarman and I did a scene from one of his great movies *Best Friends* to pay tribute to him and Goldie Hawn.

Spoofing Star Trek beaming down to Jupiter's Burt Reynolds Theater.

We took pictures with the creator of that incredible program, and it was time to go and bring in the next elite team of apprentices.

Burt and our 1986/87 Apprentice class

35

Hey Burt … it's M-A-R- … Say it!

What an amazing year! What an adventure! What great friends I made, plus a work ethic second to none thanks to the legend, Burt Reynolds. But Burt … would you please please, please just say M-A-R- Mark! I thanked him for a fantastic year; I was a lucky guy for more reasons than one. I was going to meet the girl of my dreams Because of Burt …

... MY WIFE

Andy Kato, who today runs Burt Reynolds old theater as the Executive Director of the Maltz Theater, was Julie's roommate back then and set us up in November of 1986.

She was a very talented waitress, and I was an actor. We only dated a few months and decided we were going to get married on March 14th, 1987 and head straight out to Los Angeles. What are the odds of that working out?

I could understand why anyone would think we were nuts, but we loved each other, shared the same values, wanted kids and wanted to eventually have a family, so what the heck ... we might as well do this.

Julie was/is naturally pretty. Athletic and hardworking, she was not high maintenance and didn't rely on makeup to take her an hour to get ready.

We had a great wedding, and I had a terrific support system. To save money, we had no honeymoon and literally started our fantastic journey. Before we left, Julie's Uncle and Aunt (Bill and Connie Harris), gave us their credit card to pay for hotels and gas on the way to Los Angeles and that was their wedding gift. Very supportive, creative and helpful. We stopped in St. Louis to say goodbye to my mom and stepdad, and that was pretty emotional.

Julie and I were off to the unknown, nervous, but determined. Seemingly, the whole way there, I was convincing Julie that everything would be okay. As we approached the bright lights and massive congestion of Los Angeles at night, I became overwhelmed and afraid and literally wanted to head back. Julie said "Nope. We got this". Thank God she said that because I would have turned around.

Being an Artist is very much like being a professional athlete. One must be extremely self-disciplined, focused and if they are in a relationship, the balance of all of it is oh so crucial. I remember saying kind of a "prickish" thing to her before we were married to see if she could handle it … "that show business will never take you away from me, but you can't take me away from show business." I said that because I tried other things in life and at that point, there was nothing else I could do. There was no backup plan, so it had to work.

That was our agreement going into this insanity, so we both had to figure out how we were going to manage.

What kind of a person would have the courage to go with a guy, with no honeymoon, no job, and one car to travel across the country to try to achieve the impossible? An incredible person that's who and her name now was Julie Fauser. Her story will be throughout the book, but for 32 years she has been my All-Time Leading Lady.

Burt had taught me the ups and downs and the work ethic needed to survive, and survival was at the forefront of our minds. Although Burt and his school had tried to prepare me, this was real life, it was time to start at the bottom and see if my training was ready for the real deal. Did I have what it takes? How low could I go and survive? We were about to find out Because of Burt …

… BLOWING MIDGETS

Yup. My first job in Los Angeles was blowing midgets.   Don't worry; I'll explain. Thanks to Joanie Burton, one of my apprentices from Burt's school and fellow classmate, hooked us up to be production assistants on the film *Garbage Pail Kids*. Since Julie and I only had one car … Julie would drive me from Brentwood to the valley (which was about a 45 minute drive one way) at 5:00 am, and my job was literally to take the animatronics mask off of the little people and take blow dryers and "blow them" or cool them off because of the tremendous heat inside the masks. Being a production assistant is one of the hardest jobs I've ever had. We worked non-stop and were yelled at all of the time because the frustration gets trickled down to the bottom, and the job I had was at the bottom. We were the last one to eat and the first one done from eating and one of the last people to leave the set. We didn't have cell phones back then so when the day was done; I would call Julie on the landline to pick me up. It was often 15-hour days, and I would have to wait 45 minutes for her to get there and then drive home 45 minutes and do it the next morning at 5:00 am again, all so you can get screamed at and blow little people.

Joanie and I laughed a lot because the pressure was through the roof, and it was the only thing you could do to make light out of our situation. How did we go from getting college degrees, Burt's theater, getting paid professionally to act and now blowing little people? It was a non-union movie but had actors in it like Anthony Newley and Mackenzie Astin.

The little people were good actors too and nice. The 2nd A.D. was riding my ass a lot and for no reason. I was working my butt off, and this was a power thing with this guy who always yelled at me. I finally blew up and was ready to deck him and the director Rod Amateau stepped in between us and had me sit at his table for dinner. It was such a classy move on his part because he knew I was giving him everything I had and more to help him succeed. By having me eat at the top dog's table, nobody ever messed with me again, and all I wanted to do was work harder for Rod. I then went from blowing little people to video assistant, and then they needed me to do the slate.

Rod knew I wanted to be an actor and so he rewarded Joanie and me for our hard work and did the old catch-22 to help us get our SAG card. You can't get a SAG card unless you are in a movie, and you can't get in a film without a SAG card.   I will always be indebted to him.

The non-union crew went union and all of a sudden, I went from $250 a week of being a virtual slave to 1,500 dollars, and life became a lot easier on all counts.

One memory I had as a naive newbie on a Hollywood set was that although it was a rated G movie … one of the young girls who was supposed to be in a hot tub was asked to take all of her clothes off. Now I know in the theater we have quick changes, and it's all business backstage, but to sign up for a rated G movie and find out you have to be naked on film that will last forever. I could tell she was utterly compromised and mortified. I knew that Rod wasn't a perv; it was just something that he thought was natural … meaning we probably would not see she was naked, but I could see her mind racing.

"If I don't take off my clothes I could get fired, but if I do take off my clothes the whole world could see me naked, and I am not prepared for that."

I remember saying, "Hey isn't this just a rated G movie? Why can't she wear a swimming suit?"

I was too naive to realize that it was entirely inappropriate for me to speak out with my ranking on the set, and yet it was utterly inappropriate if someone didn't speak out. I can vividly remember her mind ticking about what she was going to do. She was at a fork in the road, and I quickly realized that these kinds of things happened all of the time, which was very different from any other job I encountered in the Midwest. Rod, was completely cool with her wearing a suit, so no harm no foul and the young lady thanked me afterward.

On the last night of the shooting, we had all of these models in bikinis who were in a scene where all of the *Garbage Pail Kids* would be chasing after them. The movie wrapped, and there was this big after party with bikini-clad girls everywhere. Julie picked me up, and the next morning I came in to clean up after the party, and there were naked models and naked little people everywhere. It's truly amazing what people think can get them ahead in life. At least I only blew the little people with a blow dryer. Lol.

Doing the slate on *The Garbage Pail Kids* with McKenzie Astin.

I was fortunate to get that job and forever thankful to Mr. Amateau for looking out for me and getting Joanie and I our SAG cards. Something even better would come along Because of Burt ...

... THE HIT SQUAD

Remember Tommy Thompson, the sound guy who Burt helped at the dinner theater? He and his wife, Jan, came out to Los Angeles around the same time we did. Rene Valente, a producer, who I met at Burt's, offered to produce a showcase for my fellow apprentices and me. Everyone seemed excited. The same old material that everyone did in Los Angeles, was not something I wanted to do, so I talked to Tommy to see if he and I could write scenes for everybody.

Tommy agreed. In fairness to my friends, neither of us had credits or a proven track record as writers. They were respectful but just didn't have faith that was the right way to go, so the showcase never happened. As luck would have it, Tommy landed a TV series as a writer because of Burt, and guess who Tommy hired? ME!!!

Kelly Monteith was the host of *The Hit Squad*. My main job was setting people up on camera without them knowing about it, very similar to *Candid Camera*. Although I was acting, it was mostly improv.

I had a story outline, and an area I had to keep the people in, but it was basically me trying to push people's buttons.

Julie would see the shows too, and they were not always easy for her. One time I played the boss of a company and told the "victim" that I had concerns people were taking things from the business, and that I needed them to watch monitors throughout the workplace to see if anything inappropriate was taking place. In the meantime, I was in my "office" chasing around my "secretary" (actress) in my underwear, and the "victim" had to decide what to do. Tell me, her boss, that she saw me in my underwear chasing a secretary or pretend it didn't happen.

Now imagine for a second doing that for your job and having to explain that to your wife. "Honey, I'm sorry I was just kind of chasing a secretary around the room .... In my underwear ... but it was no big deal!" It's not like you could act like nothing happened because it's going to be on television for her and the whole world to see. You take that and me doing a scene from "Butterflies are Free" in my underwear for a USC project at the same time, and you could imagine things weren't going well at home. I didn't want to be with anybody but Julie but blowing little people and chasing girls around in my underwear were not getting me brownie points.

It was not looking good for either of us. I was basically the sole provider, but what I was doing was hard for Julie to handle. But that was part of the "dream," so what was I supposed to do? I would not do a nude scene or anything like that, but what were we going to do to survive?

Just in time, Julie found us an apartment managing job! Although we had free rent, we had 28 units to try to keep occupied and take care of.

There would be other survival jobs that would come indirectly Because of Burt ...

... SURVIVAL

My friend Stacy Sacco, who also worked for Burt Reynolds Dinner Theater was now in Los Angeles to work as an executive assistant for Thomas Bahler, a successful musician. Through her position, Stacy would get other apprentices and me odd jobs to survive.

Michael Deal from Burt's Theater and Patrick who was Charles Nelson Reilly's life partner were able to get two jobs and hire me as their assistant. One was for a movie called *Matters of the Heart* with Jane Seymour. I remember again being a fish out of the water. Michael and Patrick were great and protective of me, but would point at a guy and say, "Tell that bitch to get her ass over here!" I was like "Her? What am I missing?"

They would say, "She's a mess that one. I need her to bring that prop over here right now!"

This went on for two days, and finally, I said, "Guys, why do you keep calling he a she?"

"Because she's a bitch. You'll learn about her and others the more you're out here." Then Patrick said, "You know that Bruce Jenner is a woman?"

Now keep in mind this was in 1990, and I said, "Yeah right. I'm telling you, you gay people will do anything to strengthen your numbers." LOL. Boy did they call it or what?

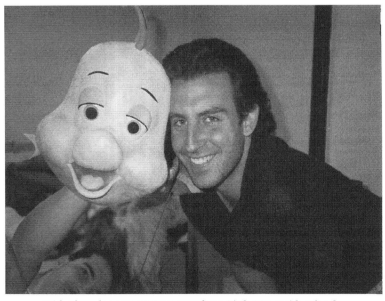

With Flounder a Henson muppet from *Little Mermaids Island*.

They knew so many things about so many people. Like who was gay and the important things like who was a facephiliac. I said, what the hell was that? They told me stars who liked looking under a glass table at people pooping. My education from being this naïve kid from the Midwest kept evolving. They then landed a TV series called *Little Mermaids Island* which was a spinoff of the movie. We had Jim Henson making the Muppets, and every episode was a mini-musical.

Burt's influence and education were paying off for many of our apprentices. John D'Aquino, with whom I understudied for at Burt's, landed the lead in his own TV series, and I was able to get an audition and part on his show called *Shades of LA*.

Tommy Thompson, my friend from the sound booth at Burt's theater, who hired me on *The Hit Squad* was now writing for *Quantum Leap*, and I was able to land a part on that show.

Jaston Williams, my director from Burt's, was doing a play, The *Foreigner* in Austin Texas with his partner Joe Sears and he asked me to join them.
I was so grateful to all of these Burt contacts for helping me get jobs to survive along with the

Joe Sears to the left as a woman, Jaston Williams in the middle and I behind him with this talented cast to do *The Foreigner* at the Paramount Theater in Austin Texas.

apartment managing job that Julie and I were doing.

I was hired to do an original musical called *Jump Rope* with several of Burt's apprentices, and Dom's wife, Carol Arthur. The show had potential, but the first-time director was in over his head, so Carol called Dom to fly in to rescue us. Dom took over and the show and was well received.

Although I was surviving, there were so many more talented and gifted people than me who just stopped. Maybe the saying is true ignorance is bliss and if so, I cornered that market space.

As apartment managers, Julie and I would show vacant apartments, deal with repairs and complaints, clean, vacuum, maintain the rooftop jacuzzi that would often leak into an apartment on the 4th floor. We would have to clean homeless people feces on our property ... yup, it was pretty crappy. But we were surviving. Julie taught at a private elementary school too and sometimes catered at night. One of the waiters she worked with was a struggling actor who was ready to call it quits.

This struggling actor got a traffic ticket and had to go to a school for a day and there next to him was the executive producer of a new show that was going to get shot called *Home Improvement*. The producer took to the struggling actor and gave him a shot, and he landed the role of Al Borland .... His name was Richard Karn. Think how that traffic ticket turned his life around.

With Sheryl Crow at Mizzou and later neighbors in LA.

As a teacher, I would never recommend you get a traffic ticket to get a job, but that is the crazy nature of the business. You never know who you will run into, who could change your life overnight.

I ran into an old friend from college who I discovered lived literally right down the street from me. She was hugely talented at Mizzou, but after graduation, she taught music at an elementary school. On a lark, she went into a blind audition and nailed it. It was to sing back up for Michael Jackson, and my friend, Sheryl Crow landed the gig.

During the survival times, Dom DeLuise would often contact Julie and me and made us feel like we were part of their family. Like we belonged.

Again, I can't stress the importance and the value of "Contacts." Contacts are often earned from hard work and sacrifice and usually only then do those contacts go to bat for you.

When I first arrived in Los Angeles, Dom invited me to an audio facility where he was doing the voice over for the movie *Spaceballs,* in which he played "Pizza the Hut." This required him to watch the screen and wait for the three-beep countdown to lay in his voice to match the movement of the mouth of the monster on screen; of course, he was fabulous.

What a valuable lesson and how thoughtful that Dom was kind enough to include me. I can't begin to tell you how much that meant to me. He and his wife Carol would call us, and I would hear Dom's voice on my answering machine as he invited us to his house. When I was down or doubting this journey, I would listen to that call over and over trying to convince myself that I belong.

Two of my great teachers and friends Dom DeLuise and Charles Nelson Reilly.

We would be at Dom's house, and it was as if we were just part of the family. There was the legendary Mel Brooks, Terri Garr, Julie Hagerty, Ruth Buzzi, Carol Kane, and Charles Nelson Reilly. There was so much laughter everywhere and enjoyment. The food that Dom would make was outstanding. His talented sons, Peter, Michael, and David, who were like my brothers and then there was Mark and Julie Fauser. Dom would have me do my imitation of William Shatner for Mel Brooks. It was surreal, it was homey, it was comforting, it was a moment in time every so often that I felt like I mattered.

Keep going, Mark. Hang in there. Keep fighting.

With the Legendary Mel Brooks. What a great guy!

As apprentices, we all liked each other and missed the training, so I went to Charles and begged him to teach in LA, offering to run the school for him.

Charles found a place, and I collected the money and recruited key students for the other classes. Although to Charles it was not about the money, his time and commitment needed value. Everyone was happy to pay it and honored he would teach us.

On several occasions, I received a call from Charles Nelson Reilly to meet him for dinner at his favorite restaurant called Adriano's, an Italian place that was costly and is now closed. There would usually be a group of us … a few celebrities and a few of Burt's apprentices.
I looked at the prices and freaked.

"Don't worry about it. It's a free meal! Get the lobster."

I never had lobster before and can't stress enough how much it meant that a pioneer and teacher was kind enough to pave the way for me and give me a taste of what it could be like. He paid it forward and encouraged me to do it too. Another time he called, and I met him, there was Burt Reynolds.

It was the first time I had seen Burt since we graduated, and I was quite sure he didn't know who I was because he never said my name. We were at dinner with several people.

"Mark, do your William Shatner," Burt suggested. I nearly fainted. Burt Reynolds said, my name. He knew me! He fricken knew who I was. I could not have been more thrilled; in that one moment in time, years after I graduated, Burt Reynolds finally said my name. M-A-R-K.

Burt's apprentices were working left and right. My buddy Jack, who almost dropped out of the program, was hired for a role in Burt's movie *Breaking In* …. That was great! Burt hired Tommy Thompson to write an episode for *B.L. Stryker*. Incredible. He employed other apprentices like Gigi Rice, who met her husband, Ted McGinley, at Burt's too. He hired 15 other apprentices that I know of to do *B.L. Stryker*. Fantastic! In addition to hiring them, he employed half of Jupiter Florida and brought all kinds of stars to his home town to help their economy flourish. They were all working and getting jobs. Another apprentice, Eddie Driscoll, was hired to do *B.L. Stryker* too. Wonderful! He also scored a role in Burt's Movie *Physical Evidence*, that's "Wunderbar!" Burt also put him in the movie *Breaking In* … WOW! Burt flew Eddie to New York for an audition. He bought him a car. He what??!! Now hold on a second! He bought Eddie a vehicle? I was happy when Burt finally knew my name. I was starting to think my bar was way too low. Wait a minute!! What was I thinking??! Our gift was getting a first-rate education from a Hollywood legend and his many friends. Over 140 of us in ten years received our equity cards and how dare I wish for more. I had no right to expect anything else.

Sadly in 1989, Burt's many gifts and generous offerings were written off against the Theater (and often those gifts had nothing to do with the theater), and due to money, he closed his baby! Our baby! The place where we all met, learned, worked and created our life-long bond.

I felt so blessed to get an excellent education from Mr. Reynolds and had a fantastic opportunity to see how hard and yet how much fun the business could be. It was great to see my peers get the call from Mr. Reynolds to appear in his many shows and movies, and although I was very happy for them, I wondered if I would ever get the call. I questioned myself. Was I not good enough? Did he not like me? Mind tricks happened all of the time in the industry, and the best thing one can do is be prepared like a reliever on a baseball team. Just keep the **FAITH** and be ready to go if and when the coach would call your number. One day during the first season of *Evening Shade* I received a call to audition for a role, and my life was about to change all Because of Burt ...

... EVENING SHADE

In March of 1991, I received a call from the office that Burt would like me to audition for a part on *Evening Shade* during the first season. WOW! This episode was written by my college friend Patrick Sean Clark, who may have had something to do with my call which is the beauty of having friends in the business.

After the audition, the director, David Steinberg, commented that he liked my choices. I was thrilled to get the part, although it was not a big part. In the world of television, that's not the point. You need credits to build up your resume and reel. An added bonus was that it paid nicely for the first episode, a replay earned you the same amount, and reruns paid forever as well.

You also get credit towards your health insurance. More importantly, I was in the game on a hit show.

On the set the next day, Burt Reynolds actually came up to me! Giving me a big hug, he said, "Hey Mark, how are you?"

My role was to play a jerk reporter in an episode entitled, "I Am Wood Hear Me Roar." Mr. Steinberg started the scene, and I was killing Burt's character with kindness. Burt stopped the scene and said "I thought he was supposed to play a jerk? Burt immediately figured out what I was doing and said, "Oh I see, you're trying to reel me in and then ... (to himself jokingly) shut up and just play it out, you schmuck."

We continued the scene, and I turned on him. It worked. He lovingly gave me a hug afterward and said, "good job." This time I was so happy to hear "good job" ... without the do over's from class and the "Burt Love Clutch."

We talked about Charles Nelson Reilly's class that I helped organize and several of his apprentices, and we clicked. My good friend and fellow apprentice, Pepper Sweeney was Burt's personal assistant on the set, and he helped create a family environment with all of our classmates.

Julie and I had a good friend from the dinner theater, named Scott Jackson, who was now working in Burt's office. Scott's a great guy, funny, kind and had a small role in one of my favorite movies *Caddyshack*.

Scott came to our wedding, and like many people, I have to thank him for looking out for Julie and me. The next week, I received a call that Burt wanted me on the team, as a production assistant. I was so grateful. Getting on the MTM Studio lot on a daily basis definitely gets you back in the game.

I worked on the show with incredible joy and would do anything to help it succeed. It was a real family. My teacher Burt Reynolds had a hit show on his hand with an All-Star cast and a fantastic writer/director producing team with Linda and Harry Thomason. I was so grateful to be working with them. By the end of that year, Burt Reynolds won an Emmy Award for Outstanding Leading Man and was nominated for a Golden Globe. He earned a People's Choice Award and Michael Jeter, Charles Durning, and Elizabeth Ashley were all nominated for an Emmy. Linda Bloodworth Thomason had another hit show on her hands that was in the top 20 and sometimes top 10. I was gainfully employed on a CBS television series as an actor/production assistant, and my role was about to change going into Season Two Because of Burt …

... EVENING SHADE SEASON 2

Pepper Sweeney, a former apprentice, was not only Burt's on-set assistant but as Burt did to so many people, he created a role on the show just for Pepper named Neal Heck. Burt knew that Pepper, in addition to being talented, was a good-looking guy and with him being younger would help gain viewers from a younger skew. In addition to acting on the show and being his assistant, Pepper would often play Burt throughout the week when Burt would direct. It was so cool to see my buddy getting this wonderful experience. I have always been on the outside looking in, but now I was actually in the foyer with a massive house of opportunities to still explore.

While being a production assistant, I was still writing, acting and running Charles Nelson Reilly's school.

I think Burt knew I did the school for free so I could help all of our team, including me …. while also serving and paying Charles to do what he loves.

Being a working actor gave you leverage and Pepper, perhaps because of his time with Burt on *Evening Shade,* helped land a lead on a new NBC Television series called *Round Table.* Pepper was going to be on an Aaron Spelling show, so the outlook was bright. For Burt, this was just another one of his many kids who he invested in that was succeeding.

My wife Julie and I were having our first baby in September of 1991 and around that year, after Season 1, I received a call from the office that Burt wanted to see me. I was escorted to his dressing room, and we sat around and ate Reuben sandwiches from Jerry's Deli on his floor and talked football. He loved football, and so did I. We were like two kids creating our favorite All-Time best NFL teams. I asked him who would he have at QB?

"Unitas and Bradshaw."

"How about running back?"

"Jim Brown and Walter Payton." We then started putting up pictures of him and various stars throughout the room. I did the same thing at my house to remind me that I worked with these great stars before, and if I did it once, I could do it again. It also reminds you of the good times in an up and down industry, but Burt had a gazillion pictures to put up.

"Let's move Dolly over here." Burt would say. So, I would get the picture of he and Dolly Parton, and either he would hold the picture, and I would hammer or vice versa. Along the way, he would share his affection for these iconic stars. He shared how much he enjoyed working with Dolly and how talented and funny Goldie Hawn was. His love and respect for Dinah Shore and Sally Fields. Burt had such respect of history and the greats from the past, but he was also a complete gentleman about the female stars and women he dated. Burt had a lot of respect and affection for his co-stars and the women in the industry. He was not one to use his power to get a woman (which was unsettlingly familiar in the business by others), but that's not to say that there weren't mutual relationships.

There was this mixed guy who I could tell at times just wanted to be the stay at home, "normal," family guy and the other side of him was to accept the role he was cast as … the sex symbol. The two naturally don't work well together.

"Hand me that picture of Angie Dickinson." As a young actor, I looked at that picture of her naked on top of him in a movie they did, *Sam Whiskey.* I asked my teacher what do you do in a situation like that?

"What do you mean?" He said.

"I want to be respectful to my wife and the actress, but I am human too. If that were me, I would be fearful that my private parts might get a little jumpy and stand at attention."

He laughed and said "that is just a part of the business and if you are respectful the woman understands. It is what it is." He reminded me, "It's not comfortable for anybody.

Having all of the people surrounding you in the crew, while you have to be aware of the camera and your objective. Plus, you're often friends with her significant other, it's just not as exciting as you think."

He then completely contradicted himself. I was guilty of watching movies with Loni making out with someone else and said, "Did you really have to do that to him?" We laughed so hard at his admitted hypocrisy.

"Hand me that picture of Clint." Boy did he love Clint Eastwood. The two stories that kind of linked them together were first when Burt and Clint were on a studio lot and were fired on the same day. They told Burt they fired him because he couldn't act, and they told Clint that his Adam's apple was too big. Burt jokingly told him, at least I can learn to act, how are you going to get rid of that Adam's apple? A second story was when they were on the movie *City Heat* in a fight scene; one of the actors accidentally used a real chair instead of a prop breakaway chair and damaged Burt's lower jaw. A relatively unknown disease back then called Temporomandibular Joint Disorder (TMJ) gave him vertigo, sensitivity to light, sound, and throbbing pain to the ears and jaw, all of which made him lose an incredible amount of weight. He was bedridden almost for a year. Burt reminded me of all of the tabloids that wrote him off for dead because they thought he had AIDS. Nobody knew Rock Hudson was gay, and when he announced he had AIDS and died in 1985 the whole world learned not only about the deadly disease of AIDS, but many linked it to being a "gay disease."

The industry knew Burt Reynolds had many gay friends, including one of his best friends Charles Nelson Reilly, and many wrote him off to be the next victim to AIDS. "Some people thought I should distance myself from Charles and my other gay friends for the sake of my career and I simply would never do that. My friends were my friends, and they came first." I found that so refreshing and my love and respect for him grew exponentially because his values there were just like mine when it came to friends. Ironically later that year, Magic Johnson would announce he had AIDS and dispelled any and all rumors that AIDS was a "gay disease."

Looking back at that time in his life, I started to understand Burt's movie choices. In the era of his rumored demise from AIDS, it seemed like Burt would never give up his friends for a rumor in the tabloids and industry. In my opinion, he tried to overcompensate to say "I'm not dying - look how tough I am" with a string of movies like *Stick, Heat, Malone,* and *Rent a Cop.* Those types of films were not playing to Burt's strength, and it is one of the dangers in Hollywood when you are in that stratosphere ... who do you listen to? Who do you trust? What do the fans want? What do the studios want? What does your agent want? What do you want? There is no playbook to figure it out.

Burt gave me a twenty-dollar bill, to get some more nails. When I came back, I gave him the nails, receipt and his change and he looked at me funny, and I said, "Did I do something wrong?"

"No, I'm not used to people giving me change back." The money he had made throughout his career was astronomical, but how much did he just give away because of his tremendous generosity and heart? I came to learn a lot.

Burt told me how much he loved his former student Pepper and how proud he was of him. He then asked me if I would be his personal assistant on the show since Pepper was leaving.

After all those years of questioning whether he knew my name or not! To know all of those years how happy I was for my peers for jobs they received Because of Burt. I wondered if it was in the cards for me and did I belong and now the old saying, was true … "Good things come to those who wait." I was the next man up, and I gratefully agreed!

We didn't have cell phones back then or texting so I couldn't wait to get home to tell Julie. I was spending several hours with Burt Reynolds, having a blast. We really clicked, and I was going to be his on-set personal assistant. Whooooooo! I was floating with joy, but we still had more pictures to hang.

"Hand me that picture of Robby Benson." I would often hold the picture up, sometimes higher than I could reach, while he judged if he wanted Robby there or not or if it had to be over a little.

With Robby Benson and Julie

He told me a funny story about Robby Benson, (voice of The Beast in "Beauty and the Beast" and a heartthrob) who not only would act on our show but would direct several episodes. In my opinion, Robby is the dream star. Polite, grounded, not caught up in the whole hype … a true artist who loves his family passionately. Robby worked with Burt before, and it was a pattern you would consistently see with Mr. Reynolds being loyal to his friends.

Burt said he invited Robby to the house for dinner and when he opened the door there was Robby with his wife and kids and his dog that came running into the house too.

Burt loved Robby, his wife, and family, but wasn't expecting the whole bunch, so he had to adjust to make more food which was fine, but why would he invite his dog? Especially an obnoxious dog that was running throughout the house barking nonstop. Was this dog going to piss and poop all over his house? What if it breaks something? It was anything but relaxing.

They all sat down trying to eat, and it was tense. Everyone felt very uncomfortable with the dog's terrible behavior barking and running up and down the stairs driving Burt nuts. He knew how polite Robby was but didn't understand why he didn't do something about his dog.

Finally, Burt couldn't take it anymore … "Robby, I invited YOU to dinner and love that you brought your family, but why did you bring your dog?" And Robby responded,

"That's not my dog, I thought it was yours." The tension was gone, and so was the dog. It was so fun to be able to hear Burt's classic laugh throughout the night.

We were talking about the real tough guys in the business. Not just the ones who played tough in the movies but who were really tough in real life. "Robert Mitchum was incredibly strong." During "Lucky Lady," Gene Hackman locked a guy in a bathroom on a jet and wouldn't let him out. Charlie Durning and Jack Warden were tough. They boxed against each other and were both two of the nicest guys, but if you crossed them (and it would take a lot), they were killing machines. Charles Bronson, Lee Marvin and of course John Wayne were all tough. I loved Star Trek and the way William Shatner fought, and he didn't disagree. The old TV show, *The Wild Wild West* fight scenes with Robert Conrad were some of my favorite. Burt liked Robert but said they were at a party once and got into a fist fight over something so stupid he couldn't remember. He described the tussle kind of like the movie fight he had with Joe Kapp in *The Longest Yard*. Two tough guys just going at it forever with neither willing to stop until others broke them up and both of them laughed it off.

I liked Clint Eastwood movies and Clint in those roles, and he agreed. *Sharky's Machine* was great, and I applauded Burt's choice to be so vulnerable and real. Burt appreciated it. In *City Heat* … Burt was classic Burt and Clint was classic Clint, but I couldn't help but ask the hypothetical … if Burt was to get in a real fight with Clint who would win? He paused, and then said "Clint was strong, but I was faster, and I would fight dirtier. So, I would win because of that." He then gave his classic laugh.

Burt and I had so much fun that day – which started around 3:00 in the afternoon and were now about 1:30 am.

My first day as his personal assistant on the set was to protect his jewels. Yup! My job was literally to make sure his kittles and bits didn't come out for all to see in a two-part episode called *Three Naked Men*. He was basically nude with a short piece of flesh looking material covering up his boys that would pop out periodically. I would politely point, and he would adjust, and we laughed a lot.

In addition to that, when Burt was directing both episodes, I played his role until he was ready to actually shoot. What a pleasure and honor to act and work with these incredible actors.

My job was to be an actor for Burt when he was directing. I would run lines with him throughout the week so he would be ready to shoot as an actor. I would do my best to help him stay on task, per his instructions for his incredibly busy schedule, and with everyone and everything pulling him in many directions. It was personal to try to get him to know his lines and kill it which was the primary reason we were there. Burt encouraged me to give him any and all ideas as another creative voice. In addition to that, I would often spend endless, enjoyable, educational hours by my teacher in the editing room with him. I would get him food and drinks, be his eyes and ears on the set and give him moral support throughout.

He would also allow me to sit in on meetings to just learn that part of the business which was simply priceless.

Let me set the stage for you what it was like to be on *Evening Shade*: As for the cast, we obviously had Burt; his leading lady was the lovely Marilu Henner, Burt's sidekick was the hysterically funny Michael Jeter. His other friends on the show were the great character actor Charles Durning, the honorable and noble Ossie Davis, the classic Hal Holbrook, the whirlwind Elizabeth Ashley, and the breathy Ann Wedgeworth to name a few … seemingly every week some new powerhouse celebrity was a part of the *Evening Shade* family, and it was all led by Linda and Harry Thomason, who had mega experience in this space of the sitcom world and were both extremely kind and generous to me.

A typical week would look like this: On Monday we would have our table read with the cast to discover what worked and what didn't in the script. Afterward, the director would start staging the actors, so they knew where they needed to be within each scene.

The writers would go back to their room and create new lines, pages, and sometimes entire new scenes. Tuesday the actors received the new pages and incorporated those changes with the director's help. The director would report to the writer's pro's and con's, and the writers would write more. Wednesday was the network run-thru so CBS would watch to make sure they were on board with everything along with the writers. If they had changes, they would be incorporated often. Thursday was camera blocking – so the crew knew what they were shooting and where. We had a 4-camera shoot which was a luxury back then. Friday, during the day, was practicing everything we did on Thursday in a more fluid form and adding any last-minute tweaks. The live studio audience came in at night, and we had a stand-up person and a band whipping them into a frenzy. Then we introduced the cast and did our first scene a few times and then the entire script usually in chronological order. Sometimes the actors took breaks and interacted with the audience. It was an actual show within a show. We would do this about 3 weeks out of the month with a week off.

The MTM lot was filled with an array of a virtual who's who of A-list talent. Burt's office was right across the hall from Jerry Seinfeld's office. Almost daily for 4 years, we would see Jerry, Larry David, Julia Louis Dreyfuss, Michael Richards, and Jason Alexander.

Roseanne Barr's show, the *Roseanne Show,* was closer to the entrance and we would see their cast as well. For a while, there was a mini - on the lot feud between Tom Arnold and Julia Louis Dreyfuss. Tom once parked in Julia's spot and she or someone put a note on his car asking him nicely not to. He responded by taking a Xerox scan of his butt and put the image on her car. Tom came in and told Burt with great enthusiasm what he did, but I could see Burt didn't think that was funny. We had *Cybil, The Larry Sanders Show, The New WKRP,* and several other shows on our lot.

Hollywood often gets a bad rap. Being that it is comprised of emotionally talented gypsies who hop from job to job, the one thing I always note is while artists and industry people are on a set, one does their very best to create a family-like atmosphere to protect those around them.

Case in point; I was part of the *Evening Shade* family and my wife, and I were about to have our first born and needed health insurance. Harry, Linda, Burt and the writing team didn't flinch from putting me in as an actor, which provided me health insurance to take care of our son. How classy was that? Burt was directing an episode called "*Tying the Knot.*" His character was to get a vasectomy, and I was to play one of his former students to come to the hospital room in a small town and unknowingly embarrass him. I thanked Burt, Harry, and Linda so much for the opportunity and the gift they gave me, but this was just who they were.

Burt knew I was connected to most of the apprentices and if there were roles, we could fill with our family of friends he would ask me who is doing what. I would throw names out to him to see who he wanted or who might be right for upcoming parts. He loved his students.

Michael Jeter, my little Nick, and the lovely Linda Gehringer.

On September 16th, 1991, my wife Julie had our firstborn, Nickolas James Fauser. What a joy. What a dream come true to be able to work on a top 10 show for CBS and have a beautiful wife and son at home. Sometimes I would bring Nick to the set, and he was always greeted with great affection. Marilu was so sweet to my son and was anxious to have her own kids. I think Burt felt a sense of pride knowing that I met my wife through him and now we have our first son Because of Burt.

We shared a lot of kid stories about my new son and Burt's new adopted son Quinton. Burt had a picture of the *Wizard of Oz* in an expensive frame that he gave to me for my son Nick signed Uncle Burt.

Shortly after that, I was cast in another *Evening Shade* episode called "*The Road Trip*" with semi-regular on the show Hilary Swank, who was not only so lovely and talented but also went on to be an Academy Award-winning actress.

Getting this acting job, in addition to my regular gig, helped greatly with credits, extra money, and getting badly needed insurance for the following year.

With Academy Award winner Hilary Swank

In addition to that role, *The New WKRP's* office was by ours as well, and I developed a friendship with Bill Dial, who was their showrunner and executive producer. A huge fan of Burt's, he cast me as a firefighter. Again, more money, more acting credits, more going towards insurance, more fun all Because of Burt. Burt was pulled in so many different directions not only for the show but other meetings, movie scripts, public service announcements, autograph signings, more meetings and he loved buying gifts for people through catalogs. He would lovingly brag to me about his son, and he and Loni would often visit us on the set. I took my job very seriously and wanted the show to be successful. The writers would check with me throughout the week on how his lines were coming, and as a writer myself, I felt a huge responsibility to them. I would be on the other set shooting my part, and when I wasn't, I would run back to check on Burt and make sure he was doing okay. Burt was kind, generous and proud anytime his kids worked, and I was now convinced I was one of his kids. There were times where we had to work on lines, but generous acts from him would distract him from our tasks – like … specifically, one week he was passionate about getting the Florida State Football team all new uniforms that he helped design for a big upcoming game.

I could not get him to study because he was too busy giving. He wound up buying the entire football team two sets of jersey's home and away, and I forgot what the price tag was, but it was astronomical.

He didn't want credit, he didn't want notoriety, he just wanted to help his friend Bobby Bowden and his Alma mater look great. Buying things for people, was the norm for Burt. It was almost as if Santa Claus was based on Burt Reynolds. He bought me a watch, a pocket knife, really expensive lamp shades, belt buckle, shirts, clothes and they were just random acts of kindness that overwhelmed me.

I remember seeing a new house that he was looking at. "What is that?"

"It was a new house I just bought for my sister Nancy."

"You just bought your sister a house?" He looked at me as if to say no big deal. He hired his stepbrother Jim for our show and on many many movies. Jimmy Lewis was one of the first apprentices, and he hired him to work on the show in the camera department. An AD that he fought for was Marla Bradley, who was in my apprentice class. Helping her become an assistant director was a complex catch-22 scenario too. You can't get in the Director's Guild unless you work a union show, but you can't work a union show unless you are in the Director's Guild. He did the same thing for Dale Stern and gave him his break with the DGA, and now Dale is winning Emmy Awards as a successful director. Countless apprentices came through our doors to work. Burt showed me jewelry, paintings, etc.… that he would buy to surprise Loni. Cast members and crew members were recipients of his gifts all of the time. He had a massive party at his house to which I was invited. Betty White was there, as well as Robert Loggia, Charles, Loni, and Dom. It was truly unbelievable how many people loved Burt Reynolds and how much he loved others.

Jimmy Hampton was best known for his role in *F-Troop*, but Burt had him in the movie *The Longest Yard* and played Caretaker. Because of Burt … Jimmy was writing on *Evening Shade* and directing episodes. Burt hired friends, like Charles Nelson Reilly and Robby Benson to direct. He had a wonderful long-standing relationship with our director of photography Nick McClean, who had a tremendous body of work. One of his last shows was the television series *Friends*.

Nick told me recently, every time he opened up his garage door in his beautiful Malibu home, he says out loud "Thank you, Burt." Burt simply loved to spread his bigger than life heart to everyone because that was Burt Reynolds.

We did another show that season called *The Thanksgiving Show* with a relatively unknown actor at the time … Billy Bob Thornton. He was a standout performer and would score big in large part because he was funny, but Burt was one of the better reactors. By that I mean, as a leading man, he served as our point guard – his reactions to the people around him were instrumental assists to help the other actors score. Billy was so kind to me. We shared a bond through our love for St. Louis Cardinal baseball. Little did I know how vital Billy Bob Thornton would become to me in the future and that was all Because of Burt.

Bill Clinton was great friends with the Thomason's, and he would come to the set. Who would have thought he would soon become the President of the United States?

Although I was there to be Burt's personal assistant on the set, Burt and everyone knew my primary goal was to act and write, but until that break would come, I would always commit to my job there and be forever committed to Burt.

One day, I was in his dressing room, hanging out like always, and I told him about a script my best friend, Rich Petrofsky and I wrote called the *Blue Crew*. It's a comedy about the first female umpire to make it to the majors and the powers that be wanted her to fail, so they stuck her with three of the worst umpires Bill Murray, Dan Akroyd, and Albert Brooks. Burt loved it and contacted Tom Mount, the former President of Universal Studios. Boom! Just like that he picked up the phone and called the former President of Universal Studios. Are you kidding me? This guy oversaw *Animal House, Back to the Future, ET, The Blues Brothers, Best Little Whorehouse in Texas* and of course Burt's blockbuster *Smokey and the Bandit*. Tom was successfully producing movies like *Bull Durham* and *Can't Buy Me Love*, and Burt called him and pitched the idea. Tom Mount read our script and loved it. He gave us some great notes to address, and we did the changes. The next thing you know my friend, my teacher, my boss Burt Reynolds just optioned our movie *The Blue Crew* with Tom Mount as his partner.

Burt Reynolds had a terrible experience on *Saturday Night Live*, but he really liked Bill Murray and had a ton of respect for him. Ironically, one of my good friends then and now is Joel Murray, Bill Murray's brother. Joel and his wife took my wife and me once to Bill's Malibu home to hang out, and there were stacks and stacks of scripts. Joel really liked my movie too and could totally see his brother in that role. That meant a lot to me, but something I learned from several people is that for a star of Bill Murray's caliber … there would not be enough hours in life to read all of the material he was given. Usually, with stars, financial offers had to be given first for anybody to even consider it and that kind of serves as a weeding out process. Again, a catch-22 because without Bill Murray saying, "I would like to do this," you have to depend on two unknown writers to sell your movie which is likely not going to happen.

Tom Mount was a great salesman with mega credits and experience as well as Burt, but Hollywood has an odd way of stereotyping and labeling people in a far different way than I would. I looked at it like Burt knew the business because he was the number one box office star for 5 years in a row and Tom knew the industry because he was the fricken President of Universal Studios. Hollywood looks at it as "WAS" is the keyword. What's now? What's selling now? Burt Reynolds WAS a major movie star, but in their mind, he was JUST a television star then. Tom Mount WAS the President of Universal Studios, but the last few movies he produced didn't do as well as others, and that is how Hollywood labels are placed on very talented people. I found it unsettling but factual for Hollywood's belief system. For me, Burt Reynolds was a movie star who was also a TV star and at any time could do both. C'mon, Hollywood; right is right and wrong is wrong, and what I saw with those labels was just wrong. Oops, I forgot. Right is not right and wrong can be right if you are the bigger star!

Hollywood, in this case, was the bigger star. A bigger star than Burt, a bigger star than Tom Mount, and by far a bigger star than Rich and me. Imagine the hurt Burt Reynolds felt knowing that … and trust me he knew he was then viewed as JUST a television star. He was once in the front row at the Golden Globes, and during our time there he was in the back row because he was JUST TV. No way he could ever do movies again. Can you say "Boogie Nights?" LOL. You tell me who was right.

I have to skip a decade later to share a story that relates to this. Brent Briscoe and I were told that a major Studio wanted to do another *Vacation* movie with Chevy Chase and the whole original cast … but they wanted Chevy and Beverly D'Angelo to basically pass the torch to the daughter or son (with a significant other) to be the leads to a whole new franchise.

Many writers in town pitched to the producer with the rights, and after a long process, they picked Brent and me. We spent two months watching all of the movies and carefully crafting an original script that would incorporate everything they wanted. We went in to pitch to the studio and before we even opened our mouths the buyer who wanted it questioned whether Chevy Chase could still act. What?!! Do you know how insulting that was to me? Chevy Chase was a major movie star!!! You don't forget how to act!! How disrespectful to actors! How disrespectful to have every writer work on pitches (per the buyer's request), and then we get selected as the final writers to present our pitch, and he questions whether Chevy can even act? Right is right and wrong is wrong, and what he did was just flat out wrong. The end result again was I was wrong! Right is not right and wrong can be right if you are the bigger star! He was the Studio buyer and was bigger than the producer, and the writers.

Anyone who could be the President of a major motion picture studio and have the successes Tom Mount did plus many of his own movies would always command respect in my book, but it just doesn't work that way for them. Needless to say, it was optioned and later optioned two other times by two different producers but never sold. YET! It's never over, baby!

That season on *Evening Shade* was a magical year! The show was nominated for a Golden Globe, Burt Reynolds won a Golden Globe for Best Actor, and when I showed up for work, CBS/MTM honored him at the gate and within the studio.

When I saw Burt on the lot, I screamed and ran towards him and jumped into his arms like a pitcher-catcher who just won the World Series.

In addition, Michael Jeter was nominated for A Golden Globe and won the Emmy Award, and Burt and Charles Durning were nominated.

We had a fun party where our two leaders, Burt Reynolds and our creator Linda Bloodworth Thomason, set the stage as a real success story.

As the Los Angeles riots hit, things became tenser, and tension would spill onto our set for Season 3 … but again I was lucky to get a front row seat of all this Because of Burt …

... EVENING SHADE SEASON 3

Over the summer, Julie and I moved out as apartment managers after 4 years and moved to the valley to be closer to the studio. I worked in Burt's office on his behalf to man the fort while Scott Jackson went down to Florida to work with Burt on the movie *Cop And A Half*. I would take care of his mail, field all calls, but would be able to be home with Julie and my son Nick.

Burt was into producing more things whether it was movies, made for tv movies or other television series and there was always something happening on proposals, etc.... While at work, I would get hundreds of autograph requests that we would stack up and honor when Burt would get back. I would field calls from stars, producers, Loni, friends, and calls almost daily from people who wanted to talk to Burt about his old jaw disorder TMJ. There were hundreds, and I mean hundreds of requests for not-for-profits wanting Burt to make a public service announcement or sign a script for auction items. Every day, I would talk to Scotty to see how it went on the set with Burt and give them updates from the information I received that day.

While there I had several people call to see if they could use our *Evening Shade* theme song for their wedding that Snuff Garrett wrote. Many called to see how they could get the song. It was not something readily available back then because there wasn't Itunes or Amazon. So, I would try to help the people get a copy of that music.

When Burt came back, one of the first things he told me was that he had a new theme song for *Evening Shade*. "What?" I told him how many times our theme was requested over the summer, but I could tell the ship on that sailed. Bobby Goldsboro worked with him on a theme that Burt liked. If Bobby did it within Burt's company, Burt would get a piece of that action if the song went big. That made good business sense, but to me, it didn't make artistic sense. That other song was just beautiful. It was an excellent underscore for sweet moments, and it was one of those rare signature songs that every series wanted. If something is not broke why fix it? To Bobby's credit, he won an award for his theme song.

My understanding was that Burt was not the happiest camper on *Cop and A Half* and was often highly agitated. I'm not saying that it was right but I could only imagine what Burt was feeling during that time. "I was the biggest movie star on the planet, and I could do anything I wanted. I could be the tough guy, the funny guy, the nerdy guy – anything ... but his tough days were coming to an end in the movies.

Burt Reynolds was fricken tough in real life, and if he could project toughness and anger, he would do it as much as possible. That wasn't what made Burt so endearing and loveable. Burt had a heart of gold, he was a lover, he was sensitive, he was funny. So funny. He was a great storyteller, and I go back to what a brilliant reactor he was … which is an art form that must be studied. An actor who is a great reactor sets everything up for everyone. Jokes, moving moments he was so good. He often told me what made Johnny Carson so great was he was a great reactor to his guest. "The guest would not be funny unless Johnny said so with his expressions or laughter. If Johnny thought you were funny, you were funny, and that is what made Johnny Carson so great". That gift that Johnny Carson gave many was something that was passed to Burt.

He loved being the lead on *Evening Shade* and making those around him funny and many times at his expense. I can't tell you how underrated Burt was as an actor for being such a selfless reactor to other actors. I beg you to watch the movie *The End.* The scene in the hospital room with Dom DeLuise and Burt Reynolds was amazingly funny. Burt was the great reactor to Dom's brilliant acting. Burt's reactions to Dom's character spinning out of control upped the ante.

The other tricky thing Burt was dealing with at the time was the death of his mom. He loved his parents dearly. Like James Dean, who was always seeking his father's approval … Burt was very much like that and would often tell me "My dad never told me he loved me." When his dad was around, I often had a front row seat to witness just how proud Burt's dad was of him, and that he most certainly did love him. Burt was grateful I saw that and shared it with him, and it was one hundred percent true.

Linda Bloodworth Thomason was very aware of this too and wrote a special episode for Burt called *First Heroes* which was loosely based on his father. Burt directed it and respectfully speaking … he might not have been the best person to direct this episode because it was deeply personal to him. I would, in the most respectful way, encourage his performance and yet per his instructions to be his eyes and ears, encourage him not to push so hard. I think there becomes this natural, only human thing for actors that if one wins a Golden Globe and an Emmy, they better really do well in an episode the following year if they want to win another.

And if you win another, you become a bigger undeniable star which means you have more power, which means you get better material and more clout to have that power to get it done. The next thing you know you are doing things for all the wrong reasons. As Charles and Burt would say … just do the work, and the rest will come, but it's easier said than done. It's easier taught than implemented.

Linda, who was the creator of the show, made some changes that she thought were best. Burt and Linda had a massive fight on set which hit the tabloids, and it mainly caused Linda to lessen her involvement with the show, which to me was not a good thing. Right is not right and wrong can be right if you are the bigger star! Linda was the bigger star in the television world, and there might have been some tussles and public disagreements on her show *Designing Women* with some of her actresses, but it was never in question who was in charge - Linda. Linda was very much a pioneer in our industry.

Everyone in the industry knew that the creator and executive producer was in charge unless the star was bigger and, in this case, Burt was a bigger star and impossible to replace. We were better and stronger with both of them, and I knew it, and Burt knew it. One of the things that I witnessed is that when Linda would write an episode, she often had it percolating in her creative mind and did it when she was inspired and backed into a corner. I can be like that too, and many artists are. I would ask her husband Harry does she have it ready yet? Harry, "Nope, but she'll get there." Nobody can question her brilliance, but from a practical matter, the actors would often get a 40-page script two days before they were to shoot it. For some of them like Charles Durning, Ossie Davis, Elizabeth Ashley, and Burt it wasn't as easy to memorize all of that word perfect for that format. As a writer myself, I knew how much time writers spent wordsmithing, carefully crafting strategic arcs for the season and seeing the long 30,000-foot view of the series to sustain itself for many seasons. Burt came from a world in the movie business that scripts are like suggestions and property bought and owned by the studio. Hopefully, they say what's on the page, but are often encouraged to throw out alternatives and create their own witty dialogue which at times works and other times doesn't. That is completely opposite from the television world. The words matter and the writers want to hear their collective words heard because they know where the show is going.

This was a problem which had been brewing for a while and that I feared would eventually come to a head. They were two different worlds clashing with not enough compromise from either side. I was/am a writer who valued/s writers and the tremendous time, energy and creativity they put into a season.

The writers and creator basically are responsible for creating hundreds, if not thousands, if not millions of jobs across the world, including; marketing, accounting, distribution, networks, different languages and remixing for different countries. I was/am an actor, and it's my face and reputation out there. I don't want to look like I am trying to memorize lines at the last minute as they spew out. I want to know it so I can honor the writer and then forget it so I can just "BE." Unless you were in each other's shoes, it's difficult to understand. I know Linda was not an actress, and Burt was not a writer, so I did my very best to give them both my perspective to show the value of the other side.

Looking back at this time, it took a lot of balls, arrogance, or ignorance to have the courage to honestly speak my mind to both of them. I would like to believe that they sincerely knew I cared for both of them, had a great deal of respect for both of them, and was motivated to do the RIGHT thing for the show. I wanted them both to succeed.

During this time, Burt made an incredible compromise. He purchased a device that would go into his ear so I could feed him his lines by the book while someone else was talking. That's a hell of a compromise, but Burt was a team player and did it. He wanted to keep it under wraps and not tell anyone and try it to see if it would work.

Basically, he was the Quarterback, and I was his offensive coordinator calling in the plays. It was hysterical. Burt told me, "If for some reason, I don't hear you, I will pinch my nose or go to my nose for something, and you just give me the line again."

So, we studied the script together and went over the lines, but during rehearsal, we tried it, and Burt was doing great. I fed him his next line while someone else was speaking. Nobody knew. I was sitting much farther away, so nobody would hear me or see what I was doing. As the week progressed, we knew this system would work and kept it under the radar, but later during a scene, he had with Marilu, while she was talking, I fed Burt his next line and turned the page. As she responded I fed him his next line and he said it. Marilu looked at him funny, and Burt pinched his nose, and I fed him his line again, and Marilu stopped and said: "You skipped a page."

Burt looked at me and jokingly and lovingly yelled: "You putz"! He started cackling with his classic Burt laugh, and he let the cat out of the bag. He shared with her and the writers about this device that worked when his assistant wouldn't be dumb enough to turn two pages accidentally instead of one. ☺ It was a system we often used throughout the year, and during shows, I would sit near the monitors on the floor with the writers all huddled around me trying to give them my best word inflections to feed to our Quarterback and star, and it was utterly surreal. After takes, the writers would congratulate me when Burt would nail it.

Linda and Harry became passionate about another show they were producing with John Ritter, and my buddy Billy Bob Thornton called *Hearts Afire*. Markie Post was on that show and her husband Michael Ross was a writer on our show. By Linda and Harry producing and creating this show again, they created more jobs for our camera operators, hair and makeup people and so many more. Harry and Linda were also spending a lot of time with the Clintons in Washington, doing their best to get him elected as the President of the United States.

Harry and I had many talks about right and wrong, and he was a tremendous mentor to me as well. One thing he told me that I will never forget was "If you think Hollywood is bad it's nothing compared to Washington politics." "There was nothing dirtier." It was so hard for me to believe that Washington was dirtier than Hollywood. How unsettling that my friend and boss from the Midwest was now trying to help his friend navigate through dirtier waters than Hollywood.
Needless to say, I think Harry and Linda were instrumental helping Bill Clinton win the Presidency. If memory serves correctly George Bush was leading in the polls, and during the Democratic convention Harry and Linda wrote, shot and edited a piece about Bill that was merely a game changer. It was polished and beyond Hollywood slick. I never saw anything like it for either party. It showcased how likable and charismatic Bill was and yet didn't look political at all and humanized him as the everyman. From that point on his approval ratings jumped and never looked back. Bill Clinton became the President of the United States, and I genuinely think in large part because of Harry and Linda's creative magic behind the scenes.

Burt, nor I liked that Linda was not around as much because her talent and Harry's were greatly appreciated by both. To some degree, the tension on the set decreased dramatically (not because of them but the mixture of everyone together that was never ironed out) and perhaps for that reason that was a good thing.

I want to share with you my experience working with these incredible actors that I saw on a daily basis Because of Burt …

... MARILU HENNER

With Marilu Henner

An enjoyable, energetic person best describes Marilu Henner. She has a unique super autobiographical memory that allows her to remember exact dates and moments throughout her history. Well-read, a walking computer bank of knowledge was Marilu, while at the same time being hip, cool and sexy. My first few years on the show she was extremely flirtatious in a kidding and respectful way too many of us. It was harmless like the way I flirted, or Burt flirted, and we just had fun. We talked about her friendship with John Travolta where I would get to do my imitation of him for her.

Burt directed many of the episodes over Season 2 and 3 which meant I was able to play Burt throughout the week. There were times where the script called for us to kiss ... but I was just the stand-in and felt it would not be appropriate for me to kiss the star. One time, Marilu wore a skimpy, sexy outfit during dress rehearsals which would require us to be in bed together.

Another time, we were in Ossie's restaurant for a scene and were supposed to kiss, and of course, I did not, and Marilu jokingly stopped the scene and said, "Burt, I have been working with Mark for two years, and he never kisses me." Everyone laughed, and I think I blushed, but even though she was joking, I was not going to let her call me out without getting even with her.

The next time we did the scene I dropped my script and planted a big kiss with her. She just went right along with it, and everyone laughed. It was utterly harmless and all in fun with a friend I valued.

She was very loving to my wife and newborn son. She would hold my little Nick and would jokingly tell me that she wanted a baby with her husband. It wasn't long after that that Marilu was pregnant and I was so happy for her.

Another thing that Marilu was very conscious of was her diet. Her parents passed away at a young age, and she was confident that diet was a huge key to avoid illness. You certainly couldn't argue with her health and looks. Marilu was always in a good mood and a very uplifting person. She was low maintenance and a perfect team player to have on our team.

Marilu and Burt loved each other as great friends. He couldn't have spoken more highly of her, and I know that I was blessed to spend 4 years with her and watch her beaming with pride when she brought her son into the world.

After the show was over, Marilu had her own talk show. She had Burt, Charles, myself and a few of my apprentice teammates on to honor Burt.

... OSSIE DAVIS

Ossie Davis was a soft-spoken beacon of love. He was wise, unflappable, and genuinely sweet. Ossie was inspirational to me because he was an actor/writer as well. He encouraged me to keep doing both. He was married 57 years to Ruby Dee, (a classy lady) and a great role model for me. Ossie did his art and balanced a great marriage, and that is precisely what I wanted.

I believe his friendship with Burt was the longest of anyone on the set and his loyalty to Burt was clear and yet aligned like mine. He would not placate to Burt because he was the biggest star. He wouldn't tell Burt what he wanted to hear but told him what he thought was best for Burt and always do the right thing. Burt would tell me how much that meant to him when Ossie would do that because Burt knew Ossie's heart was in the right place and genuinely loved Burt for who he was. The Los Angeles riots were unsettling to me. We could see the fires burning from our apartment rooftop. What kind of world was I bringing my son into? Haven't we advanced as a country? I explained my angst to Ossie.

He was my Yoda, my Obi Won, and he calmly and logically explained to me as a kid how the Klan threatened to shoot his father, how he endured racism as a kid and in the business and how close he was to Martin Luther King Jr. Ossie put his hand on my shoulder and lovingly said, "We shall overcome." It meant so much to me because in my heart he was saying "collectively together we shall all overcome." That the soul and spirit trumped skin color and those who understood it collectively win and create the beautiful world we are all capable of having. Those who don't get it will fight and fight and waste valuable energy on hate. If anyone in the world had the right to be vengeful and bitter for all of the racism and discrimination he encountered, it was Ossie Davis, but his alignment with his friend Martin Luther King Jr. proved to be a far better tool to get results ... LOVE. Have the Dream and imagine that world that we all deserve and can become.

... MICHAEL JETER

Michael Jeter was our go-to guy. If we needed a joke or lacked funny, Michael Jeter would get the call. He could milk a laugh like no other, and I mean, milk it. Sometimes I would watch in awe as he would extract every last ounce of juice out of the joke and would know how to move on to the next. As Charles Nelson Reilly would point out, Michael was not only a master in his delivery of lines but could fill the white on the page as very few could. He was our equivalent to Barney Fife on *The Andy Griffith Show*. He was a relatively unknown actor throughout the country but highly respected in the industry. Michael won a Tony Award on Broadway for his work in *Grand Hotel* and, of course, won an Emmy for our show.

Michael was unpredictably moody, and one never knew what to expect. 70 percent of the time, he was the light-hearted, fun, loving guy everyone wanted to hang with. Michael was always the consummate professional, but sometimes he would be in a dark, sad, mad place that was never personal to anyone else but there was no consoling him. He wanted to work it out by himself.

He shared with me that he was molested at a young age and that often haunted him. I felt so sorry for him but also started to see a similar hurt too many of my gay friends that were also molested. So unfair for any kids to endure that at a young age. What the hell is wrong with people? Needless to say, his real pain, was channeled into helping other people in the world smile, be enlightened, and moved. He was a beautiful soul, and I was honored to call him a friend.

... CHARLES DURNING

Charles Durning was one of the greatest character actors of all time. Whether he was singing and dancing in *Best Little Whorehouse in Texas* or his wonderful role in *Tootsie* when he thought he was in love with Dustin Hoffman as a woman. The man was a brilliant actor. For his size, he was incredibly nimble. One might think because of his weight he would be a pushover, but he could smile at you, shake your hand, calmly twist your thumb and have you on your knees in excruciating pain.

He was a war veteran who shared with me about having to fight a German soldier on the beach of Normandy in hand to hand combat. Knowing one of them was going to die, he shared with me how bad he felt, but it was killed or be killed. He won 3 Purple Hearts and a Silver and Bronze Star for valor. It was not something that he enjoyed talking about, but Burt loved Charlie and was proud of his service.

There was a great friendship between him, Burt, Charles Nelson Reilly, and Dom DeLuise that we would all be at various parties and I felt so lucky to be included in this iconic group.

... ELIZABETH ASHLEY & HAL HOLBROOK

Elizabeth Ashley played a very good thorn in Burt's character's side. She was perfect for the show and excellent in her role. Elizabeth and Burt had great chemistry and a long-standing relationship. She was a whirlwind of a person who could turn on a dime and tell you to go F off but would leave you uncertain as to why she said that or what you did to warrant that. Before you could figure it out, she had moved on to something else. My sunny disposition as Elizabeth writes about in the picture did not always fair well with her exasperation. However, she was valuable to the team, and that was what it was all about. Burt told me "if you went to war, you want Elizabeth Ashley in your foxhole because she will fight to the death for you."

Working with this 4-time Emmy Award winner, Cable Ace Winner, Academy Award-nominated actor daily was a thrill too. Hal was Charles Nelson Reilly's peer in acting class when they started out around my age. How inspiring it was to all of us young students to see how they stuck together and succeeded. Hal Holbrook was friendly, kind, egoless and a team player.

... GUEST STARS ON SEASON 3 OF SHADE

Terry Bradshaw and Greg Gumbel were on the show playing themselves, and Burt was particularly funny in this show. The history of Terry and Burt from various movies was cool, but also talking to Terry about the Superbowl he played against my all-time favorite player Jack Youngblood was a real treat.

With Terry Bradshaw and Greg Gumbel

Both Terry Bradshaw and Bernie Casey were ex-NFL football players that Burt loved and hired several times throughout his career. "Ava Takes A Shower" was a 2-part episode starring Reba McEntire and Vince Gill. Both were incredibly kind, humble, and flat out good people. This was the beginning of more things to come for Reba and me, all Because of Burt.

With Bernie Casey

Many apprentices were hired. Alice Ghostley played Mrs. Hannigan in my first Equity show at Burt Reynolds Theater, and I was able to work with her again on *Evening Shade*.
Richard Simmons was on our show and a complete delight.

Bob Denver was a guest on our show. He was such a big star in the '60s. Huge! He was the lead role on *Gilligan's Island* at a time when there were no residuals, but because of his recognizable face, he was virtually impossible to cast for anything.

Burt was very sympathetic to Bob and very protective of him because he knew the hardship of the business and Bob was typecast. Imagine the fame, the money, the success Bob Denver reached at a relatively young age and as soon as *Gilligan's Island* ended it would be hard to make a living or be accepted as anything other than Gilligan. How do you budget your life that way? How do you peak at 30 knowing the rest of your life is downhill? Burt instilled in me that "**EVERYBODY MATTERS**" and I had a lot of respect and appreciation for the years of entertainment Bob Denver gave me.

With Bob Denver.

The great Florida State football coach Bobby Bowden and dear friend of Burt was nervous and reluctant to do the show. Burt told me to focus on Bobby and help him with his lines. I tried to calm him, but the whole thought of acting was not his gig. He was not going to say the writer's lines because it was a foreign world to him. Since Mr. Bowden was playing himself if the coach just knew what his intent was, he would be fine. He did great.

With Bobby Bowden Coach of Florida State Football Team and close friend to Burt.

The writers gave me my favorite role on the show playing a Mr. Haney like sleazeball salesman that many small towns have in an episode called *"Bring Me The Head Of Carl The Mule."*

WKRP called me again to play a funny EMT. That doesn't just happen if I'm at home in my apartment, it's because I was on the lot and saw executive producer Bill Dial who had a role for me. It's Because of Burt Reynolds ...

In our apartment complex was an incredibly handsome youthful looking friend named Scott Wolf that I would bring to our basketball games that I would organize on Saturday's. Scott looked like a young Tom Cruise and had a great personality. I felt that if Burt Reynolds met him, he would like him and help him.

Brent Briscoe and I were doing a play *The Right To Remain Silent* and I suggested to Scott he should come because I knew Burt would be there. After our show, I introduced them, and sure enough, Burt asked me to bring Scott to the studio for lunch the next day. Scott came, and Burt incorporated him into our show *Evening Shade*. Burt Reynolds did it again. Scott needed a break and Burt gave it to him. When you were on a show, you not only have exposure, money, credits and more chance of health insurance but you also have leverage. From his appearances on *Evening Shade* and knowing we would bring him back the following season, Scott was cast as a lead role in *Party Of Five*. Scott, was very talented and had a terrific look, but does that break happen at the time without the leverage? Could his opportunity and break have come Because of Burt…? I think it did. When Scott landed the break, Burt paused for a second because he created a role for him, but literally beamed with pride that another one of his assists went on to bigger things. That was who Burt Reynolds was.

I watched how Burt spotted talent, and I learned a lot from him. There was this pretty girl on a set right next door to ours. I had never seen her before, but virtually every day she would have lunch in the commissary at the same time I would. I would watch how she would interact with everyone. She was so much fun, personable, and beautiful. I watched her relatively unknown show on TV which was called *The Edge*, and I pointed her out to my wife. "See that girl right there. She's going to be a huge star." Her name was Jennifer Anniston. Later, she would have a significant impact on my life, and I am sure she doesn't even know it, and I will explain that in the *Waking Up In Reno* section.

I had so much fun that season. Burt Reynolds was nominated for a Golden Globe award, and Ruby Dee and Michael Jeter were nominated for an Emmy Award.

I was acting with Burt Reynolds on *Evening Shade*, I was acting on *WKRP*, I was Burt Reynolds, personal assistant on a top 10 television series and feeding lines in the ear of one of the biggest stars of all time. I had a play *The Right To Remain Silent* that Brent Briscoe and I wrote that was playing in Los Angeles that we also acted in. *The Blue Crew* was optioned, and I had another movie I wrote called *Home Field Advantage* optioned by Rene Valente. I had health insurance, a beautiful wife and son, how blessed could one be? Yet there would be so much more all Because of Burt …

... CONVERSATIONS WITH

Conversations With was a CBS series that Burt did to interview iconic people in the business. In the first episode, he was able to secure the legendary Jimmy Stewart, Mickey Rooney, Van Johnson, and Ricardo Montalban.

I met Ricardo several times before, once at Burt's Theater, but at a few parties and would always do my Captain Kirk with him. So much fun!!! I also was so moved by Mickey Rooney's portrayal in the movie *Bill*. I wrote a role for him in my movie *Home Field Advantage* because of that.

Burt knew of my great affection towards Jimmy Stewart and guess what Burt did for me? He had me become Jimmy Stewart's personal assistant for the day. Oh my gosh! I wonder how many flies I caught that day with my mouth agape? I watched *Vertigo*, and *Harvey* on DVD the night before and told Mr. Stewart how much I enjoyed them. He wasn't aware that *Harvey* was on DVD. He was one of those rare old school high character people who could balance the two worlds of wife/family and the high-pressure demands of the business.

I met him on the CBS lot on a golf cart that would take him in the building, to the elevator and to where we were to shoot. The elevator was not happening quick enough for his liking, so he wanted to take the stairs. I felt terrible that he was going to march all of these flights of stairs at his age, but he was the boss, and I was there to follow his lead.

With Ricardo Montalban. "Khannnnnnnnnnnnnn!"

With the legendary Jimmy Stewart.

It was a great day, where I was able to spend the entire time with one of the true legends of the business. Jimmy Stewart told me what makes a great movie is that the pictures tell the story. Very different from theater or sitcoms where the dialogue tells the story … in movies it's the pictures … and if shown well it would translate in any language.

Thank you, Mr. Stewart.

With Jane Powell and Burt Reynolds

We did another episode with female Hollywood legends; Ginger Rogers, Esther Williams, Jane Powell, and June Allyson. Classy classy classy! "Everyone matters" whether you are a struggling actor or a forgotten legend … Burt Reynolds put a spotlight on everyone.

Sadly, the harsh reality of this business was that once you gracefully age, unless there are people like Burt Reynolds to honor the past, good roles for women over 50 are hard to come by. Good parts over 70 are virtually non-existent, and in the case of two of these fabulous stars, most people younger than me will know Jane Powell for having clean dentures from Polident and June Allyson from preventing the elderly to pee in their pants with the help of Depends. Forgive my harsh sense of humor, but it is sad. It's an accurate view of the rise and fall of stars and our short memory to honor the past.

With Ginger Rogers.

With Esther Williams

… RANDY TRAVIS MUSIC VIDEO

Burt was helping Randy Travis with a music video called "The Cowboy Boogie," that I was in. Burt loved country music and the artists that made it so. Any time he could help a country artist or be a part of their work Burt was in. Those were his people. My father-in-law was on the set that day and was able to meet Randy Travis.

My father in law Jim Harris with Randy Travis

Burt saw that I was having success as a writer with two screenplays optioned, one play that he saw and scene work from another work in progress. He started to feed me the writer ball more, and it was all Because of Burt …

... FRIARS CLUB

Burt was being honored and getting the Lifetime Friars Club Award. He needed jokes to go after some of the stars on the Dais, so he asked Brent Briscoe and me to start penning some jokes for him. It was no holds barred, and everybody would be there. He wanted us to go with him and Brent, Julie and I were so excited. Comedian, Brad Garrett, was making a lot of jokes about Burt's hair and finally, Burt had enough and challenged Brad to come over and try to mess with his hair. Burt was pissed, and if Brad had moved anywhere near him, it would have been ugly. Burt knew there was going to be roasting and yet he allowed someone to push his buttons, and I was concerned for my friend. Other than that moment, the evening was filled with stars and friends, and we were so honored to be there Because of Burt ...

Burt was working on producing a spinoff series of *Evening Shade* for Charles Durning, and Ann Wedgeworth called *Harlan and Merleen*. It would also star Leah Remini and Maria Canals. Those ladies were so funny, so completely different and so enjoyable to be around. Burt asked me to help him punch up the script. One of my favorite lines I added was Charles Durning's character asking his ditzy wife Merleen to call 911.

She hurriedly left the room and then came back and asked him "What's the number?"

We received big laughs because it was perfect for her character to ask that question. One night after the show Leah Remini, Neal Patrick Harris, Burt and I just hung out. Even though the show didn't get picked up, Burt knew how to spot talent. Leah Remini went on to become a big star, and so did Maria Canals.

My wife became pregnant again, and we were excited to learn we were going to have a little girl to join our son Nick. We needed more room, so we rented a home in Sherman Oaks closer to the studio, and again this was all Because of Burt ...

Burt's dad, Loni, his brother Jimmy and his sister Nancy and Burt.

... MOVING INTO OUR HOUSE

Excited to have our second child on the way, we were blessed to find this cute modest house in Sherman Oaks.

One of my neighbors was the legendary actor Robert Morse, who many know from *Madmen*, but is a true legend of stage and screen. Robert was a Tony and Emmy Award winner and had a daughter the same age as my son. He would stop by my office, which was the garage, and we would take our kids for walks. The crazy thing about Los Angeles is that there are no bugs. I would be writing in my garage with the door open all of the time.

Burt was very excited that Julie was going to have our second child, and when we first moved into the house, he said, "Hey, you're going to need furniture for that house. Take this." He pointed to a couch. I said,

"Oh no. We're good. You don't have to do that – you've given me enough in life."

"Shut up and take it. I don't want it anymore. Really. I'm going to get rid of it anyway so you will be doing me a favor". That was Burt's way of getting me to take it. I feel confident that he was not planning on getting rid of any of this stuff but looked at it like we needed it more than he did. That was Burt. I tried to not take anything because I just didn't want him to think my relationship was what more can he do for me. He did enough for one lifetime. He said, "you're starting to piss me off just take it!". He was so sweet. I thanked him and then he did what Burt does ... kept giving. "These two cushioned chairs," "This old antique church pew bench," "I have another fold out couch that turns into a bed." "This bean bag chair." Again, I was overwhelmed by his generosity. That was Burt Reynolds! "The Giver."

Pregnant, Julie's standing by our Stage entrance.

I think there was something about Burt that he never forgot how hard the struggle was. As a great leader, philanthropist, and teacher, he wanted to give back and pave the way for others who struggled that he believed in.

At the same time, Burt had hopes that they would pay it forward.

Burt was genuine that way. He loved the world and wanted it to be a friendlier place. If anyone made it that way, it was Burt Reynolds. Needless to say, my empty house became filled with Burt's love and furniture. As I write this today, in my office are the two comfort chairs he gave me. We still have the antique bench. I have a watch, a bracelet, two lamps, and his famous Pittsburgh Steelers Jacket he wore on the show. Other jackets, sweatshirts, a director's chair … it is overwhelming how giving he was.

Burt was a huge giver … but this was just the beginning, and even more exciting things were ahead all Because of Burt …

... QUAKER STATE AND FLORIDA ORANGE JUICE COMMERCIALS

With Brett Bodine for Quaker State

Burt was offered a lot of money to be the spokesperson for both Quaker State and Florida Orange Juice. I used to work for a production company, Partners USA, that would get hired by a large advertising agency to shoot commercials for a small fortune. Burt was going to do it all. He was going to star in it, produce it, direct it and he wanted me to write it with him, and those were the conditions and they agreed.

We flew down to Florida together, and I was going to stay at Burt's house with him. I couldn't believe it. I remember being at his home in 1986 for an acting class, convinced he didn't know my name and now I'm writing commercials for him, sitting next to him in first-class, his personal assistant and am going to stay at his house.

A lot of our team went down too. Nick McClean, the great director of photographer, Scotty Jackson Burt's Executive Assistant, Jimmy Lewis, and his hair and makeup man Brian McManus. Jacob Parker, who played Burt's son on *Evening Shade* was playing his son in some of the Florida commercials. We shot a lot of this on his ranch, where I am sure Burt received location fee money too for their use of the ranch.

Burt was a gem to me as always, but his focus was not as sharp as usual. He was preoccupied, had some issues with prescription medicine (that has been well documented) that altered his mood swings. He was bothered tremendously by something at home with his wife Loni, and it was all adding up. It was on this trip I met Burt's "friend" Pam Seals.

There was trouble in River City, but I stayed in my lane. What happens between two people in a marriage are nobody's business, but I felt like my boss, teacher, mentor and friend was flirting with disaster on a few fronts.

Burt and I were pulled over by the police for speeding too. The police officer did what most people do when they see a star like Burt ... They became almost apologetic that they caught the Bandit. Burt loved police officers and was complimentary and sorry. The police officer let him go, and the Bandit got away again. ☺

Nick McClean our DP on the camera, my friend Scott Jackson in the Red Hat and me with the script on my lap.

On the Florida Orange Juice set with Jacob Parker.

We finally had to make cue cards so he would know it. That's me in the orange groves with cue cards I wrote for him.

Burt was always extremely careful when it came to stunts. It was an art form to him, and the goal was still to make it look as dangerous as possible with nobody getting hurt. That's the goal. In the Quaker State commercial, Burt was to drive into the shot pretty quick and slam on the brakes. He asked me to stand in front to give him a mark to know when to stop. I thought he was kidding, but he wasn't.

We were joking back and forth and Nick McClean our director of photography was laughing pretty hard. There's no way he could see a mark on the ground, and the shot had to be somewhat exact that his car had to stay within the camera frame, and it made sense. I trusted Burt with my life so I stood there confident he would stop well before. Burt came zipping in with the car and overshot his mark and skidded right towards me where I jumped on the hood, and it took out a few boxes and tables behind me.

I wasn't hurt at all, but Burt laughed it off, and it was uncharacteristically unsettling to me that that would happen.

If it was someone else, it could have been a lawsuit, and I was concerned about my main man. Why wasn't he more careful? Why didn't he know his 30-second spots better? It's just 30 seconds. What happens if the tabloids find out about Pam when he was playing the lead role on a family show? Again, I am not speaking out of turn against my friend, all of these things have been publicly documented. I was just genuinely concerned for him.

... CHRIS EVERT

With Chris Evert at her tennis tournament

Growing up I loved Chris Evert. It was beyond refreshing to meet my mini-crush Chris Evert in person and get to hang with her and Burt for the day at her benefit tennis tournament. Chris was as lovely as she looks. She was putting on a show for her charity and had a lot of fun with other celebrities. I knew that Burt and Chris used to date and I complimented him on how he had all of these high-profile relationships that although they ended they all remained friends. Or at least that was the perception, and I was so impressed.

Burt always talked so highly of Sally Field, (if she only knew how highly he thought of her and how many beautiful things I heard about her throughout the years). He also truly respected and loved Dinah Shore too. He really liked Chris a lot, and you could see that whatever they once had was not damaged or tainted in the least bit. The both of them were genuine friends, and that was clear, but could he recreate that with his wife that was heading to the finish line?

... LONI ANDERSON

I have always liked Loni Anderson. She has been nothing, but nice to me. Loni came to most of our shows which was a treat for our audience. One time I was at their house in their kitchen sitting at a desk, and I hear "Hi Mark," and I turn around and it was Loni Anderson in high heels and a bikini. "YOWZA" I respectfully turned my head away so fast not to gawk at the former WKRP star whose bikini poster once rivaled Farrah Fawcett's and by my quick glance noticed she hadn't lost a step. I was almost rude not looking at her when she talked to me, but I didn't want to be rude staring at her either. My thoughts were, "what the heck was she wearing high heels for in the house with a bikini on? Oh well, I'm sure Burt appreciated that. Wait! Quit thinking about this you idiot you are here because Burt needs you for something. Focus!"

Burt seemed very much in love with Loni for a while, and he was absolutely crazy about Quinton. ALWAYS! He always talked about Quinton to me and sometimes our boys would play together. As the years passed, something happened to Burt and Loni. Part of it I think was accumulative, but something perhaps more specific set Burt off. I've heard things from Burt but respectfully what happens between two people is indeed their business. His distance from her became more and more apparent by things he would say or our long hours at work (sometimes we would be in the editing room till 3:00 am). Many times, he would have me call her to leave a message on his behalf which never felt right. I didn't want her to think I had anything to do with their problems. One time we were in the car, and he asked me to call her and I did. I literally handed him the phone and said: "you talk to her."

Around this time, I knew Burt was planning to divorce Loni, and there was nothing that I could do to stop it. He had his mind made up and sometimes it's for the best.

I and others knew how he planned on serving her divorce papers, and to me, it was cruel and revengeful. This did not seem like the Burt Reynolds I knew and loved, and I was deeply concerned. I remember being so upset because this was not the best thing for Burt. I knew it with every fiber of my being and couldn't stay in my lane. I wondered why nobody else who knew what was going to happen wasn't speaking out? Why weren't they telling him their thoughts regardless of the circumstances? So, I put my ass on the line and asked if I could talk to him as a friend, and he was his gracious, kind and listened. I took a deep breath but dove in.

One, I respectfully told Burt that I was a son of two parents that I loved equally, but they divorced. I understood the anger and the volatility that accompanies a split, regardless of who was right or wrong. The one who talked negatively about the other would ultimately lose in my opinion. Because I was just a kid, and my role was to honor both of them. Someone dishonoring either of them with vitriol would only hurt their own cause.

Two, I told him how much I admired him as a fan for all those years, who dated so many high-profile women. Chris Evert, Dinah Shore, Farrah Fawcett, etc.… if it didn't work out nobody ever knew the details, they all seemed to end amicably and was inspiring to so many. It was so uniquely different than other obnoxious, hostile divorces.

Three, I begged him to consider an alternative. I suggested he produce a show for Loni. She was looking for something, and I had a sitcom I wrote based on my experience as a building manager called *Hollywood Gardens* that she would be perfect for. "I'm not saying this to be self-serving … if not this idea I beg of you to find one for her. There are plenty of ideas out there, and it would be so classy on your part to do that, and it would be smart. You can say, that your marriage had irreconcilable differences, but you are still friends, work together and share a son you both love and THAT will be inspiring to America." "Plus, you get paid instead of paying." He smiled at me, and I knew I reached him. I know he knew I was encouraging him to do the right thing and I had HIS best interest at heart.

He said he would think about it and thanked me. The next day he approached me and said, "Thanks for the advice … I really appreciate it … but I can't do it."

Selfishly, I didn't give in and said, "You can't be the leader of a wholesome family show and then do mean things to your real wife in a public way and expect the audience to not allow that to seep into their perception of you and the show."

"Mark, I appreciate your advice I really do, but I know my audience, and they'll be fine." Who was I to argue that? Who was I to debate him any further? He was my teacher, my boss, my friend. I did my job as his friend to give him my very best – to look out for him, and that was my moral obligation. It was all I could do. I still felt, right is right and wrong is wrong. Burt was a bigger star than Loni … and I should know by now that that would usually mean he would, therefore, be right, even if he was wrong. The end result was on this rare occasion … he was wrong, and I was right!

Yes, Burt was the bigger star than Loni, but the audience is always bigger than any star. They usually know wrong from right and have a way of humbling anyone no matter how big of a star you are.

Not only was serving her papers a public embarrassment that turned against him but then he did an ill-advised interview challenging Loni on television to take a sodium pentothal test to see who was telling the truth.

Right or wrong, a loyal friend would stand by you to pick up the pieces even if you were wrong and that is what I was going to do for him. I would be a horrible person to do anything else but love him unconditionally, and that is precisely what I did. He knew my personal feelings of these actions, and I addressed them to try to help. Imagine how many times my parents and friends suggested I do x and instead I did y and yet they were there to pick me up. Again, the only difference is that my MANY mistakes were not under a huge spotlight that the entire world could see.

We were collectively in a deep hole, but we were on to another movie that I was able to do Because of Burt …

... THE MAN FROM LEFT FIELD

I met Reba McEntire on the set of *Evening Shade* and as big of a star and talented as she was she was even more beautiful than that in person. She was a mega country recording artist but was interested in acting more. Her natural approach combined with her wholesome persona and attractive looks made this a no-brainer.

Burt loved all kinds of artists, visual artists, stuntmen, photography, actors, all arts but he loved music. Burt had a sincere heart for country stars and the people in that industry. Those were his people, and it was a mutual love affair because they loved Burt too.

He really believed in Reba, and if you look at his track record of spotting talent and fighting for them, he had an excellent success rate. He wanted Reba to be the star of this movie called *The Man From Left Field* and asked Brent Briscoe and me to rewrite it. It was another catch-22!

You can't write a movie for television or a feature film with pay without being in the Writers Guild first, and you can't get in the Writer's Guild unless you get hired to write for television or movies first, so which one gives? This catch-22 discourages just anybody from getting in, and you need someone with the power to break down the door for you and again ... it was Burt Reynolds. Burt broke down one catch-22 by getting us our Equity card. The Burt connection helped break down another door, so I was able to get my SAG card. Now I am getting my WGA card Because of Burt ...

With the lovely Reba McEntire

Brent and I were so honored and so excited. The WGA explained to us as writers who rewrite you seldom get credit for revising, but you get paid, and that is a beautiful thing. Brent and I read the script and gave Burt and Rene Valente, my friend, and producer, who was trying to produce another movie I wrote called *Home Field Advantage*, ideas we thought would better the script.

As a longtime mega fan and friend to Burt Reynolds, I thought it was so cool of Burt, to want to put Reba in the spotlight. In many ways, he would be more of a producer and play this mysterious, quiet, unassuming character that would come out of his shell at the end. There was something about less is more that makes you want more of Burt – in that instance which was very appealing to me.

We came up with ways of enhancing Reba, and some of the kid's storylines better. If memory serves correctly, the original writer had Burt's character coming in at about the twenty-minute mark because he set up all of the other characters first. The writer set up the obstacles and then this mysterious man from left field appeared. It was such a bold choice, and different than the usual stereotypical here is the movie star we have to meet him first moment because he is a movie star. If that was not the way the original writer wrote it, we wanted it that way – again, my memory is not so clear on that. We wrote things that Burt was SO complimentary on. He really liked what we were doing and then called me in the middle of it and said, "Hey guy, you're both doing a great job. CBS likes it too, and if you get me an *Evening Shade* script by tomorrow, I think I can get you both to write on the show next year." "WHAT?!!!!" I thanked him profusely and told him I loved him, and he reciprocated.

I called Brent. And of course, he said, "What the F*ck! Are you Sh*ttin' me! We can't do that!" I said, "Brent this is what we were trained to do, and we're going to do it." So, we pulled an all-nighter. I mean, an all-nighter and the next morning started sending the pages via fax machine per Burt's instructions. Rene Valente called me up, "What the hell is this?! What is this crap you are sending me?" We told her it was an *Evening Shade* script per Burt's request. Of course, her whole demeanor changed, and all was good.

Burt submitted it to CBS, and the man with a heart the size of Florida did it again. Brent and I were going to be staff writers on the CBS hit show *Evening Shade* all Because of Burt …

Burt LOVED to help people, and he did it all of the time. Burt told us he was extremely proud of our work and I felt we had something different and cool for my friend, mentor, boss. Scoring a win for him was never a job to me it was a mission. I wanted the world to see what I what I was able to see. I wanted the world to see some of the different aspects of Burt that would really make him shine yet again and felt like we were close, but then he said, "I want a scene where I beat the crap out of this guy." … Ah oh. Please no Burt! Burt's anger at 57, in my opinion, was just not his most attractive quality to showcase his vast skill set.

Brent and I tried to gently steer him off that idea, but the ship sailed. He also wanted a great monologue at the end that explained his characters fog, and that made complete sense. "Oh, and I have to be introduced much earlier in the film like in the first scene." I knew this was not about the story, but about image and stardom and explained how selfless it looked that we introduced him later. How great it made him look which was my prime directive. Let's meet Reba, and see her story and the kids and their dilemma and then the miracle mystery man enters …

Burt said, "Yeah, you're right, but the fans expect to see me sooner. It is only at the very beginning, and then we get back to what you're talking about." I then knowingly lost the argument and said, something unintentionally so arrogant, I was lucky I didn't get fired.

"Okay, we'll give you that." There was a pause on the phone, and then Burt said:

"You'll give me that?" And I knew that was the first and only time I ever crossed the line with him and immediately apologized to him and apologized and apologized. He knew my heart, and it was done. But I was lucky, because although I had Burt's best intentions at heart and was passionate to bring him success, what I said, came across so disrespectful that I was lucky he didn't fire me. Frankly, as much as he gave me, he didn't deserve that.

Burt was able to shoot this movie in his home town of Jupiter Florida. Again, Jupiter was once a backwoods town before being developed into a powerhouse city. It had more excitement, more recognition, more economic boom and it was all Because of Burt. Burt was so proud of Jupiter and wanted them to get a taste of his world, and he wanted his world to get a taste of his beloved hometown.

"The camera does not lie," Burt often preached. He told Brent and I that he loved the monologue that we wrote, but respectfully speaking he didn't know it. He didn't do the **WORK** as Charles would harp on all of us about. The camera didn't lie and sadly exposed him at the end. Brent was down in Jupiter trying to feed Burt lines on our device but to no avail.

Most of him at the end during his monologue was shot behind a rock and then later in post-production he had to redo lines that just didn't work. He phoned it in and wasn't worthy of his extensive capabilities. I have seen Burt knock it out of the park with things like this before.
He was sweet, charming, loving, kind, gentle, he loved Jimmy Stewart … if he had just gone that route instead of a homeless man turning into *Sharky's Machine* roughing everyone up and then having a massive breakdown behind a rock, we would have had something sweet and special.
Burt was going through a lot in his personal life, and it affected him more than he wanted to admit. Despite those struggles, Burt was the ever so giving guy, and I was not on this set because I was shooting a Pilot for Steven Spielberg and again … it's all Because of Burt …

... SEAQUEST

Because of Burt, I met Tommy Thompson, the former soundman at Burt Reynolds Theater in 1986 while I was an apprentice. The guy who hired me on *The Hit Squad* and *Quantum Leap* and in 1993, he found himself as the head writer and executive producer on *Seaquest*, along with Steven Spielberg. Tommy knew how much I loved Star Trek and found a role for me. Weapons Officer Dalton Phillips – (I was the torpedo shooter) or Mr. Checov underwater. I was in heaven and so grateful. Tommy creatively added this role under the radar, so I didn't have to go through rigorous NBC approvals in casting. As the man running the show, he knew he could put me in all the time and build it as he saw fit.

With Shelley Hack and Don Franklin on *Seaquest*.

This was great news except for one thing. I was going to be writing for *Evening Shade* and would CBS care? Would Burt Reynolds care? Would NBC care? The first thing I did was told Burt what his former apprentice Tommy Thompson did for me and asked his thoughts. Burt loved it!

Now think about that … Burt Reynolds hired me 4 times as an actor on his show. He hired me to be his personal assistant for two years and hired me to rewrite his movie *The Man From Left Field*. He optioned *The Blue Crew* and then he was hiring me to write for his top 10 show and was willing to let me balance my acting for another show while writing his??? You talk about selfless.
I asked him what he thought they might think about me doing both and would I be disrespectful to NBC?

Sci-fi series keeps director from play

Mark Fauser was all set to direct *You Have the Right To Remain Silent*, which opened last Friday at the Burt Reynolds Institute for Theatre Training. Then something else surfaced: *seaQuest DSV*.

Created by **Steven Spielberg**, *seaQuest* is a new submarine-based sci-fi series that has the entertainment world in a frenzy. In an era when networks order series with trepidation and cancel most before they run 13 weeks, NBC audaciously ordered 22 *seaQuest* episodes.

Fauser, a 1986 institute graduate, already has shot two episodes as weapons officer Dalton Phillips. "I'm the guy who shoots the torpedoes," Fauser said.

Spielberg

Of course, it helped that *seaQuest*'s Executive Producer is institute alumnus **Tommy Thompson**. Fauser, whose credits include *Quantum Leap*, *The Hit Squad* and *Evening Shade*, wrote *Silent* with another alumnus **Brent Briscoe**.

Now they're negotiating with Showtime to produce it with an all-star cast. And they also lent a touch-up on *The Man From Left Field*, the TV movie Reynolds is shooting in Jupiter.

Fauser, who is married to another institute grad, **Julie Harris** (it's a close-knit group) hopes to check out the movie and his play before it closes May 9 … if he can get some time off.

Burt picked up the phone and called Steven "Fricken" Spielberg. Are you kidding me????? He proudly shared with him the story about Tommy and me. He told him everything and sold it while I was standing in the room. No worries. Done deal!

When Burt hung up the phone, I shook my head in utter disbelief with tears in my eyes and gratitude. "Thank you so much but why do you do all of this for me?"

"Because Jimmy Stewart did it for me and I want you to do it for others."

It was so powerful, so selfless on his part. He gave me enough and now was giving me the break of a lifetime to write for him on his show and allow me to act on another one. Drop the microphone! This man's INCREDIBLE!

The cycle of paying it forward continues as Tommy Thompson also worked hard to get our buddy John D'Aquino through and did. Think about that …

Burt Reynolds invested in these three guys at his school, and one was the executive producer of a Speilberg show, and he had two other Burt protégé's in the show. I received a letter from Steven Speilberg while he was shooting *Schindler's List*, welcoming me to the show.

The director for the pilot was Irvin Kershner who directed *Return of The Jedi*. Which in my opinion was the best *Star Wars* movie. The Director of *Star Wars* baby! I couldn't believe it!!!

Our Captain was Academy Award-nominated Roy Scheider. He was the star of *Jaws*, *All That Jazz* and many other classic movies. I walked into a large boardroom in Universal Studios to meet the cast and read the pilot episode. We went around the room and introduced ourselves. I had to pinch myself. I couldn't believe this was happening.

I loved all of the cast and crew. The set was massive and gorgeous. Darwin, the dolphin, looked so real in a huge aquarium on the set and my torpedo station was awesome with working lights.

I was lucky because Tommy shared with me his vision of what he wanted the series to be. An internal conflict between Science and the Military that throughout the season they would increasingly value each other more and more. Roy's character would serve as the mediator if you will. If that was the case … all of the subtleties that were written needed to be executed with that in mind.

The pilot was fun, and I made good money while writing *Evening Shade* in my trailer. Roy Scheider knew of my writing on *Evening Shade* with Burt, and it was an instant in and credibility all Because of Burt. Roy was exceptionally kind to me, and we interacted often.

I was loose, confident and had a lot of fun on the set, but when it was time to roll, I was all business. Irvin gave me some great close-ups and things were going swimmingly.

I was so honored to do this show and felt if we could pull this off like *Star Trek* we would be doing this for a very long time. Conventions, autograph signings, action figures (which some of the cast posed for and were made).

Shortly after that, Roy Scheider mocked *Star Trek* in an interview, and we were like ah oh! That's not good to take a shot at one of the biggest sci-fi shows of all time.

We all were called in to do some voice over work and to add some lines off camera as they were putting the puzzle together for the pilot. I remember the sound engineer being so frazzled and laughingly disgusted. I asked him what was wrong, and he said, "I played the opening of the show with President John F. Kennedy saying his famous line about the sea and some jagoff NBC Executive who had to justify his job said can we get another voiceover to replace the guy with the New England accent?" It was amazing how many jobs had to be justified by people with no talent, but that was with any business, but this one pays a lot for that fat.

From Left to Right: Marco Sanchez, Ted Raimi, an Extra, Don Franklin, Mark Fauser, John D'Aquino

The episode of *Games* was the next episode shot, and I had a pretty nice part thanks to Tommy and the writers and absolutely loved the show. Loved it!

The villain was great and played by a terrific actor named Alan Scarfe. I was blessed to be working with Joe Napolitano again who was the director of the episode. I felt so safe with Joe because we worked together before and we were all friends through Tommy. Same with the editor Michael Stern.

I loved everything about the episode, and it was Stephanie Beacham's favorite episode too. We had something extraordinary. I asked Roy what he thought about it, and he didn't like it all. In fact, Roy became very clear that he didn't want monsters, evil villains, torpedo's, fighting, etc....

He wanted to resolve everything peacefully and have the series delve more into the science and have peaceful resolutions to everything.

That would be great in real life but doesn't make for great television and conflict.

Can you imagine Roy Scheider going into the water with a wetsuit to have a heart to heart talk with the Great White Shark from *Jaws*? "Why are you trying to eat all of us? Don't you know how bad that is for the economy in Amity? What instead of eating human flesh I have Seaquest prepare you a vegan/seaweed meal that will give you the proper nutrition you need and then maybe you could set an example for all of the other Great White Sharks not to kill anymore?"

People would grab their Channel Switchers faster than Darwin could spew oxygen out of his blowhole. It doesn't work!!

Tommy Thompson was having a heck of a time getting Roy off of that, and they had substantial creative differences. How do you write an action-adventure series with no action? Right is right and wrong is wrong, and the end result was I was wrong! Right is not right and wrong can be right if you are the bigger star! Roy was the bigger star so shortly after that Tommy left the show.

Weapons officer Dalton Phillips

I hated to see my friend go who gave me this wonderful break. It just wasn't fair to him and the show and going in Roy's direction would certainly tank this excellent adventure. I was lucky to have my bigger job with *Evening Shade*. When I would get a call for me to do more *Seaquest* episodes, the *Evening Shade* writers were incredibly supportive of me, and I felt my character was still safe on *Seaquest* but didn't feel as safe.

I wanted to help Brent and get him back in the acting world, but he had no desire. I tried and tried, but he was content to just write.

Greed For A Pirates Dream was an episode where we had a situation where Roy and Don were off the ship, and a decision had to be made where military and science worked together to save an island. We purposefully played it as a collective whole with disrespect and some humor because neither science fully understood what we did in the military nor did we understand what Stephanie's character was doing with her science. Stephanie's character was asking us to fire high powered torpedo's at the island to stop the flow of volcanoes. The director liked it – we liked it, and we felt we all nailed it.

I received a call later to do reshoots. A guy named Les Sheldon was trying to figure out what to do. He wanted us to do everything non-plus. No emotion. Talking heads. I of course always want to be a team player and give those in charge what they wanted. But if I did what he said, it would be boring, and I was more than likely toast. If I didn't do what he wanted, I would be considered defiant and be toast for sure.

Wow. Not too many good choices. The first thing I did was to help Les with his lighting. We were in a red alert, and he didn't have the lights right. He checked the footage and thanked me and adjusted. If he missed that we would have had to do it all over again because it wouldn't match ... a lesson Burt taught us.

I then did exactly as he asked – I felt like it was as enjoyable as looking at paint dry. Watch the episode and see for yourself and then look on my website and see the alternative take we initially did. I think you will see it had a lot more character and conflict for all of us in the original. If you don't see a difference, then why did they reshoot it? If you like the plain one better great ... art is in the eye of the beholder, but now you know how much we care and how complex our choices are for every moment.

Roy was getting his way on everything, and the shows were not as good.

Tan and in pretty good shape back then I wanted to look good for the show. I shared a makeup person with Roy Scheider and Roy didn't want me tanner than him, so they made me lighter. I didn't want to be lighter, but they insisted. When you think about it what was either one of us doing with a tan in a submarine under water??? But when you are vain and want to look good, you find a way to justify it. ☺

Burt Reynolds was secure in himself, and if he could get someone younger and handsome like a Scott Wolf or Pepper Sweeney, he would totally do it, but Roy was competing with me.

Roy got his way with the direction of the show and our tan battle. He was nicknamed "Leatherface" by many of us. Had I continued the tanning wars I too might have been his sequel "Leatherface II." I respectfully asked Roy for an autograph picture, and this is what Mr. Scheider... The Captain on our series wrote me. "Keep the day job." Wow.

My part eventually went away. John D'Aquino followed, and other cast members left too. No more Stephanie, no more Royce. No more Stacy.

My terrific friends Michael and Peter DeLuise joined the cast in the second season and were excellent. The show moved to Florida and the powers that be overruled, Roy. The show went back to an action, adventure series and eventually, Roy left too. I think the show had great potential but *Star Trek* it wasn't. Jonathan Brandis was a significant talent. He was by far the most famous person on the show.

The sad part about showbiz is when you are on top of the mountain like he was it was great, but when you are in the valley, it is dark and scary. How does one go from that much adulation and work to nothing? The pressure of the massive highs and lows were too much, and he eventually sadly hung himself. Royce Applegate was a fun guy, and a fellow writer also and I was sad to hear of his death in a fire in his home.

With Michael DeLuise and Marco Sanchez for a mini-reunion in 2017.

Tommy will go down as one of the most helpful people to me in this business by far. He has always looked out for me, and every person I have touched in this business needs to know about Tommy ... who I met all Because of Burt ...

... EVENING SHADE SEASON 4

I was so excited to start this year in the writer's room.   We had a talented writing staff lead by Victor Fresco.   The writers were funny, kind and supportive even though we were considered "Burt's guys." Burt's public separation did not go as well as he planned and frankly, we all knew we were in big trouble. It was an excellent show, with a great cast, but the families that supported the show were now down on Burt.

Burt had a fantastic gift of knowing his audience throughout the years, but he had a rare moment of losing his perspective and quickly sobered up to the danger we were in.

I remember he and I privately talking about this in his dressing room, and he said, "How does Clint get away with so much and everything I do wrong is in the tabloids?" I could tell he was asking me from a layman's point of view and knowing I would give him an honest answer.   Burt said, "I love Clint .... He's one of my best friends, but that bastard has more ladies and scandals than I do and gets away with it?"

In retrospect, I think Burt was hugely popular and for years could go on the *Tonight Show* and wouldn't shy away about talking about his personal life.   In fact, it helped him once get cast in *Deliverance*.   But if people see you too much and know everything about you, you lose intrigue. Your audience won't need to pay to see you because you are too accessible. Clint's interviews are rare and on the topic of what he was promoting and avoids the personal stuff for the most part. There are intrigue and mystery to Clint. He is a smart businessman, who goes to work, shoots on a tight budget, gets out of town and makes the studio a lot of money.

Burt worked extra hard that year, in my opinion, to dig us out of a hole. He worked at cutting the budget and yet stacked the deck with guest stars like:

Raquel Welch ... who was his old friend, and had a unique, but a professional relationship that went way back.   When they did *100 Rifles* together with Jim Brown, Burt didn't think Raquel liked him. In fact, he was somewhat convinced she didn't like him. Sometime later, he told me she came in to testify on his behalf for something that slips my memory ... it might have been during *The Man Who Loved Cat Dancing*, that Burt had to testify based on a mysterious death. Burt gained so much respect for Raquel because even though Burt didn't think she liked him, he was so moved that she was compelled to tell the truth about Burt's character and stand by him. Burt told me he later returned the favor for her in court. Raquel was kind to everyone and stunningly beautiful but had an aura around her that was unapproachable. I could see why Burt might have felt the way he did back then, but I think that it was more in our minds than hers. Those two worked great together, and it was exciting to see.

Carol Burnett was on the show, and this was the second time I had the honor to meet her. She is an iconic comedic genius, and yet she is even a greater person. Burt truly loved Carol and had so much respect for her.

Tony Bennett, the legendary singer, was on our show ... class act.

Leslie Neilson was that funny guy you saw in *Airplane*. He walked around with a fart machine all week long and would let one rip and would blame it on the person next to him. Just so much fun and what great history to be with all of these legends.

Alexa Vega became part of our cast. Alice Ghostley also had a recurring role, the lovely Diahann Carol, K.T. Oslin, and Tammy Wynette and many others. I had a unique perspective from the writer's room Because of Burt …

... WRITING FOR A SITCOM

Being a part of the writing staff was fascinating. We worked over the summer to get a head start into shows so when we started taping in August, we would have several scripts ready and could stay ahead of the process. The first thing we did was to brainstorm the arc and direction of the show for the season. What various characters were going to go through and where they would end up. All ideas and thoughts were welcomed, debates were encouraged, and the head writer, Victor Fresco, would make the final decision.

We then started coming up with ideas for shows keeping in mind the year arc and various character arcs we were trying to get to. Basic concepts for several shows were pitched to the group by all of us. Some were tossed away, but others gained traction.

Once we had several shows that we all felt would work, we started to outline each story to see who did what and when. What situations were funny. What was our A story B story etc.... it was a distinct outline. As one was completed, we would try to outline another, then another. By the time the process was done we had several stories outlined. Once that was completed, Victor would assign individuals who he felt would best execute that script.

Once the script was done and completed the writer would submit it to all of the other writers and then they would work at rewriting, punching it up, looking for ways to better the script. Line by line, word for word and moment by moment. We could have many late nights and endless diet cokes and snacks to eat. Sometimes we would order dinner and keep going. Sometimes we would get in a rut and start playing darts. Victor would again be the final say on what goes into that script. Then we would go to the table read and hear how the actors read it. From there we would fix and find ways to make what didn't work – work better. That process was done all the way to shooting the script, and even then, we may throw some lines out for the cast to try.

We were trying to find an exciting storyline for Ossie Davis's character and, of course, someone brought up that he should fall in love which is always an obvious idea ... that seemed like my first choice too and therefore perhaps too generic and predictable. What twist could we add to that? I came up with a Hail Mary idea and so uncharacteristic of how I would envision Ossie's character dealing with this ... but what the heck. What if he fell in love with a beautiful woman who the rest of the cast found out used to be a man? At first, many poo-pooed the idea and I knew it was risky, but Victor was intrigued and overruled them.

He had the very funny and thoughtful Danny Zuker (now the executive producer of *Modern Family*) write the episode and the woman was played by the beautiful and classy Diahann Carol. Diahann and Ossie played it with such dignity, and it really worked well. The episode was called "*The Perfect Woman.*" And Diahann Carol was just that.

Brent and I loved Billy Bob Thornton's character from the show and wanted to bring him back, and, fortunately, the team agreed and let us take on that assignment.

Rightfully so, Brent and I had a lot to prove that we were not just token Burt guys. We had to work hard to deliver a good script, and we did just that. Victor and the writers were incredibly complimentary and supportive.

We started going over each word, each moment as was customary. As we prepared to shoot it, Billy Bob, who loved the script, was for whatever reason not allowed to do it, even though he was working for Linda and Harry in the soundstage next door. We were all so bummed.

Needless to say, Burt convinced his old *Smokey and The Bandit* sidekick to do our episode. Jerry Reed. Can you believe it? What great history and now these two were going to be reunited on the screen together again in our episode. Wow! The episode was called "*Educating Calvin*," and Brent and I felt we really had a winner thanks to the writers' support. We felt Burt would love it too and be very proud of his boys.

With Jerry Reed from my episode called *Educating Calvin*.

It was the Monday morning table read, and everyone in the cast and crew was there. CBS was there as was customary.

The goal was to knock it out of the park and be close to the running time, so we didn't have to add or take away too much. The cast began to read it, and it was laugh after laugh after laugh.

They were all scoring! Jerry Reed was so funny, but in large part, because Burt was such a brilliant reactor to the insanity around him. We couldn't ask for a better table read. It timed out perfectly, and the CBS executives came up to Brent and me and said: "It was hysterical and one of the better table reads we have been to." Brent and I were on cloud nine, and again we were so grateful to the writers for all of their support and of course Burt … because without him none of this happens.
I gave Burt a big hug and thanked him. He proudly loved on both Brent and I and then called Victor over and much to our surprise he said, "Jerry Reed was kicking my ass in that script. Guys, I need more jokes." We tried to explain to him that Jerry was only getting the jokes because of Burt's reaction. Burt's the one who made it funny! Without him, it doesn't work. It's kind of like Magic Johnson saying I don't want to be one of the greatest leaders and assist guys of all time anymore, I want to score more and have Kareem pass instead.

Oh my gosh, it was so frustrating. CBS loved it! The cast and crew loved it. Jerry Reed really loved it, but the man for who if not for him none of this would be possible didn't, and of course, that mattered. That mattered a LOT. He was the reason Brent, and I was there, so it was what it was. We started tinkering with what was a very tight script, and it began to fall apart like a house of cards. I remember Jerry Reed coming up to me and saying, "Why did you change it? It worked so well?" I just had to take it, and it wasn't easy. I knew Burt really well now and on any given day 95 percent of the time he would have been hundred percent good with it.

He was the one who taught me that the guest on Johnny Carson was only funny if Johnny Carson allowed the guest to be funny. Meaning, Johnny was the leader and his reactions, his looks, his laughter would make the guest shine and without Johnny doing it – it just wouldn't work. Burt knew that and yet this one time – he forgot. The show was not very good in my opinion, but of course, I am really hard on things I do. I know that CBS was confused. You know the old expression if it's not broke, don't fix it and it was far from broke. There were a lot of things broken at this time in Burt's life. His relationship to Loni, his finances, his relationship with the Thomason's and he was losing his grip on our show which leads me to the most difficult chapter to write in this book Because of Burt …

... FAME

Remember I said, I wanted to be famous because of Burt Reynolds at the beginning? I was terrified of it now and didn't want to have anything to do with fame anymore. Why? I was blessed to have a front-row seat of one of the most famous people of all time. I think Burt handled fame as good as humanly possible. Far better than I could have managed it. He was terrific, but it was all of the things that came with fame that scared the crap out of me.

Look at these extraordinary, incredible successes: Elvis Presley, Whitney Houston, Michael Jackson, Prince, Robin Williams, Heath Ledger, Janis Joplin, Philip Seymour Hoffman, Jimi Hendrix, Jim Morrison, Chris Farley, Amy Winehouse, River Phoenix, and John Belushi. That's just some of the mega-famous people who had all of the fame, all of the money, all of the talent, all of the adulation, all of the things one could dream of ... so what goes wrong?

How do these elite people die way before their time? Oh sure you can just blame drugs, but it is far more difficult than that. Far more complex. What about Princess Diana? She was famous and stalked to her death. Same with John Lennon. What about Karen Carpenter? She didn't like the way she looked and needed control over something but lost control of everything and lost her life? I say all of these things with sensitivity. These were not just rare statistics. These were real people, who were loving and talented and just wanted to entertain people.

- STALKERS

When I worked at MTM in the summer in Burt's office, I was asked to go through old boxes in the basement of the Executive Building. I found some cassette tapes and listened to them to see what they were. It was an extremely sick person casually talking about how he was going to kidnap Mary Tyler Moore and torture her. It was graphic and demented. What did Mary Tyler Moore ever do to warrant that? It was so unsettling. What would compel someone to shoot Rebecca Shaffer? Because she was famous? How about Selena Gomez? It doesn't matter how nice you are some people just don't know where the line is.

There are fantasy's that people have that they want and plot to get it all because you are merely doing your job to entertain. We saw them with Burt too, and at times we had to beef up security on the set. Burt told me one time a woman sent herself to his house in a box. When it was opened, it was not by Burt, and the lady could have suffocated.

Burt couldn't go to many events or places. He would tell me how he always had to be on guard. I was in a public bathroom once, and a fan was so excited to see Burt that Burt literally couldn't go to the bathroom and decided to hold it and leave. Can you believe it? The filter of the fan couldn't even allow Burt to go to the bathroom. I was mortified and later wrote a cynical movie using that scene in *It's All About You.*

I was on a plane with Burt going to Florida, and a perfect stranger came on board and started to berate Burt for no reason. I stood up to confront her and get her away, and Burt gently pulled me down and said, "Don't worry about it. I'm used to it." I hurt so bad for him. He did nothing wrong. He was just sitting there, and some nut job just started going after him.

Burt told me there was always someone who wanted to challenge him at bars to see if he was as tough as he appeared in the movies. Burt would try to defuse the situation at all cost, but sometimes he had to fight to survive. That is not what any of these stars signed up for, but it is a reality they have to live with. It scared the hell out of me, but that was just the tip of the iceberg.

- PREDATORS

Then you have the professional stalkers. The photographers who get paid a king's ransom for the most compromising, salacious, sexy, unattractive shot of you. They invade privacy, and nothing is sacred anymore.

We are all part of creating the monster! The obsessed fan, the photographer who will chase a person to get the picture. A writer who will write mistruths or even partial truths to sell a tabloid story at all cost is so sick and unethical, but it happens all of the time ... and then there is the public who buys it. We create the monsters! We pay for this and keep these people in business. It was so hurtful to watch story after story that Burt Reynolds had AIDS. How could someone write that? It was one hundred percent false.

I remember when the tabloids found out about Pam Seals, and that was before the separation from Loni. I learned something else ... that you could trade stories and delay stories. Meaning, Burt could not let that leak yet, so he had to come up with an equally explosive story that would help them make money at his expense. So, he told them he was bankrupt. I saw it all unfold and thought wow! What does this have to do with him being an actor who loved to entertain and help people? What did this have to do with him being this incredible teacher and giver!

Where are the stories on that? How many lives did this man change for the better? How much has he given to charities? The whole process was so educationally repulsive to me.

Not long ago a person contacted me about wanting to write a positive book about Brad Pitt. She wanted to know what he was like in college. If I were going to do this, it would be via e-mail, so I saw the questions and positively answered them way. A few questions were about Angelina Jolie and Jennifer Anniston, and my response was it's none of my business and have no comment. The next thing I know it's not for a positive book about Brad Pitt, but the tabloids used my good name for an article about Jennifer Anniston and Brad even though I had no comment on it. I was appalled, but that's how this sick world works. When Burt died the same person called me, and no way was I going to respond. I didn't want to be a part of that media circus that could twist things.

- TRUTH

There was a highly publicized fight between Burt and Linda Bloodworth Thomason. It was a heated argument on the set over re-editing his work. Burt did a Bobby Knight and tossed a chair, and the set cleared. Linda kept calling my name, and it was as if I was watching my parents get a divorce again. I cared for both of them and felt they both were trying to make the show great, but instead of talking it out – it exploded. While I was standing there somewhat between the two one of our own people called the tabloids to cash in on the story. How disgusting! In addition to having a job on our show, this person wanted more and cashed in at our expense.

There's a saying "No publicity is bad publicity." That is factually untrue. Bad publicity is bad publicity and when you are doing a family show don't do bad things that garner bad publicity or the people who crave that kind of programming will leave. Anyway, Burt was highly emotional and in near tears because it was so personal to him. The episode was about his dad, and I knew how he felt but it was he and I in his dressing room and I was looking for peace and resolution. I was honest and said. "I know you're hurting right now, and I am so sorry. That hurts me too ... but this might have been necessary because you said some good things that needed to be said. But Linda said some good things that needed to be said too."

Burt looked at me like he was going to kick my ass, but I didn't back down. I said, "She did say some good things. You two are our leaders, and if you talk this out and unite, we will have a stronger show because of it. Be the leader you taught me to be, sir." Burt's guard was completely down. He knew I loved him and would fight to the death for him. But loving him would sometimes mean, telling him things he might not want to hear at the time ... but now was the time to do it or the problem would perpetuate. Burt nodded his head and said, "you're right." Literally, within seconds a "Yes Person" who was not there came into the dressing room and said, "I heard what that bitch just did!" Then another "Yes person" - then another. I counted, 13 people came into the crowded dressing room all telling him what he wanted to hear, and I couldn't take it anymore. I said "what the hell is wrong with all of you? None of you were there?"

I was Burt's personal assistant at that time, and some of these people were higher on the Hollywood ladder, but I didn't care. In fairness to Burt ... or a famous star ... if you had 13 people you loved telling you one thing and you had another person you love telling you something else who would you listen to? To me, the numbers don't lie. But they were not there, and right is right and wrong is wrong, but in this case, 13 people who didn't hear it or see it was right because of their numbers, and I was wrong. That was the beginning of the demise of our show, and a light switch went off. There would be NO WAY if I were Burt, I could decipher the truth. I would not know what to believe.

There was another time I went with Burt to *The Tonight Show*. This was the first time Burt was going to do the new *Tonight Show* without Johnny and interact with Jay Leno. Jay was very respectful of Burt and understood the great legacy that Burt and Johnny had. The conditions were right, but the execution just wasn't there. It wasn't terrible, but nothing memorable. That's going to happen sometimes. I remember telling Burt the truth. It wasn't Burt's fault it wasn't Jay's fault it just was what it was. It was just an off night.

With Jay Leno

Burt accepted that fact. It's not easy to take when millions of people watch you – because of course, you want it to be great. I understand and am extremely sensitive to that. We went back that night to edit, and the show aired in Los Angeles at 11:30 pm and people after the show actually would show up to the editing room on the lot and tell Burt how bad Jay sucked.

The next day during rehearsals I saw people throughout the day compelled to tell Burt the same thing that Jay wasn't good, and by the end of the day, the truth was altered … it was all Jay's fault.

I shared with you the story about me confronting Burt about not trying to publicly hurt Loni regardless as to what happened between them. I know he appreciated my truth … but I can't help to wonder what would have happened if others in his inner circle would have confronted him as well. Look, that was me being young and naïve and just trying to do what was "right." But wanting to keep your job and not making waves is right too. It's a tricky balance.

Something about not living in the truth was too unstable for me, and I respectfully don't think I could handle it. As hard as I try to explain it to people, I know their initial reaction is "Yeah but couldn't they see it? I would do it differently". I said, the same thing until I had a front-row seat and realized I wouldn't know what was up or down based on everyone's ulterior motives and advise. The answer is no … the very best … the most talented … kind … the wealthiest … the most famous are all susceptible, and it's why we see so many crash or die.

- UNBALANCE

The actress Teri Garr once said, and I am paraphrasing … "When actors start out, they get treated far worse than any person should ever get treated, and if they make it big, those actors get treated far better than any person should ever get treated." It's so true! The unbalance is simply staggering. I remember starting out, and people would say "what do you do? " I would proudly say, "I'm an actor." Their look was often a grimace or doubtful snarl. 'What have you done?" they would ask in disbelief. My choice was to either run down my resume or just let them think they were right … I was a loser. When I was writing for *Evening Shade*, I remember an LA dentist pitching me stories while he was pulling out my four wisdom teeth. Yes, I was awake for it, and it was so unsettling to have someone tugging on me while pitching ideas. Think about how little an actor makes to start off and an actor who makes 20 million dollars for two months of work. That same wealthy actor will get wined and dined by a restaurant that is happy to have them in their establishment. They don't need the freebie but get it, and the starving actor who needs it won't get it because they don't matter.

Jake Lloyd was another good kid I worked with on the movie *Madison*. He was a big deal on the set with the success of the *Star Wars* movie he was in. Known as the young Darth Vader, the demands and the price were just too high. He was bullied and mocked for his role in that movie, and that hurts anybody more or less a young kid. What a shame the scars it leaves … Jake left the business and ran into some trouble. Hopefully, he will reinvent himself, find joy and be successful in whatever positive thing he chooses to do.

- TEMPTATIONS

The temptations that come to stardom are in all shapes and sizes. They can be a little pill or an expensive bottle. Something that becomes extremely accessible to someone who is famous can be an escape from the altitude of flying so high. Beautiful people come at you with the goal of getting a piece of you. A relationship, a baby, a house, a buyout, a lawsuit. When things become so easy what do you do to regenerate that high or excitement? How do you top it?

Burt was very disciplined when it came to drinking. He didn't do it in abundance, but it was well documented by Burt and others that he had a prescription drug problem that became problematic. The temptation to take a pain pill after you do stunts and sacrifice your body for your art seems somewhat reasonable, but when you keep doing it over and over again what doctor is going to tell these guys no?

- MONSTERS

There's a chance you can turn into a **MONSTER** or be the victim of one. I have seen and heard of people putting their personal needs above a movie, and to me that is sick.

A Major Actor/Director was directing a movie. They were approaching a well needed 3-day weekend, and the famous actor/director was disgusted about the footage that was shot from the dailies. It was unacceptable! He needed to reshoot over the weekend.

One of the upper people but below the powerful director said, "why do we have to do that it looked great?"

"I know, but I just need another day or so, and I think I can lay ... (that actress)." I was speechless. Why would an influential actor/director need to spend millions more and waste all of that money and hold an entire crew hostage for something he could have done on his own?

I know Burt was very sensitive towards women. I never saw him use his power to manipulate a woman or compromise one. In fact, I know he detested it and would become very protective of women who had to deal with that.

All in all, Burt was a shining example of what a star should be. He was generous, charitable, he paid it forward, he gave time talent and treasure, and I was honored to be at his side.
I just saw things that I didn't think came with the job description and I have to share it with you.

For those seeking Fame ... Be careful what you wish for you may get it and hope you hadn't. Some really nice things came along with fame though, and I was able to taste it Because of Burt ...

... THE REST OF THE 4ᵗʰ SEASON

Burt's girlfriend Pam Seals took a real liking to Julie, and although I didn't see Burt on set as much as I did the prior two seasons, we were going out more frequently at night. He would get the best tables and treatment for us at a restaurant. We would go to small private concerts and hang out at their house. Pam was kind enough to throw a baby shower for Julie at Burt's home. Julie's friends were in awe and how amazing Burt was.

I think Burt was doing a great job on the show, but again we were digging ourselves out of a massive hole because of the divorce.

In the writer's room, we would periodically get a call from President Bill Clinton to write jokes for him for various things. Can you believe it? We were working on our show, and the President would be on the phone. Surreal. Bill Clinton's brother Roger was in the band playing live for our studio audience.

On January 4ᵗʰ, 1994, my wife gave birth to our 2ⁿᵈ born Kiki Fauser. She was a beautiful, delightful girl and her brother took to her as well. My mother in law came to town to help Julie, and on January 17ᵗʰ, 1994 at 4:30 am a 6.7 earthquake rocked our world, and we were right at the epicenter. Julie swooped up Kiki who was next to her and ran downstairs and told me to get Nick. The power went out immediately and when I got to Nick's room something was blocking my way, and plaster was falling on my head. Screaming for Nick, I discovered the thing in front of me was the dresser that bounced in front of the door. Nick was unscathed and sound asleep. I took him downstairs and put some shoes on to get my mother in law who was on the bottom floor. There was broken glass everywhere, our refrigerator tipped over, it was a mess. I grabbed Julie's mom's hand and told her to get some shoes on. We sat upstairs, and it was cold because one of the windows busted. There was a fire behind our house at the grocery store. Car alarms were going off everywhere, and as I walked down the street, it was terrifying.

Julie's dad paid a small fortune for Julie, her mom, and our kids to fly to Florida while I still had to work.

Pam called me concerned because she did not hear from Burt and asked if I would go check on him and of course I did. When I arrived at his house, his front door was wide open which was uncharacteristic of Burt. I knocked on the door anyway and started to yell his name but heard nothing. Oh, crap am I going to be the one to find my friend dead? God please no. I am walking throughout his house calling his name loudly and heard nothing. Nobody is there and as I began to walk toward the front door on the couch was Burt lying there motionless. I went over to him, and blood was behind his head – I was panicked. I touched his shoulder to see if I could get a reaction and he opened his eyes, took earbuds out, as he was mellowed out listening to music and said, "Hey guy."

"Are you okay? Why is your head bleeding?"

"During the earthquake, a picture over my bed fell and hit me in the head, but it's no big deal."
The whole experience was crazy.

The next month Dinah Shore died, and I remember how shaken up he was about it at his house. As a fan, I knew of their loving relationship, and as I got to know him, he always talked so highly of her.

Burt wanted to help and employ as many people as possible within the family. It came to Burt's attention that Jacob Parker the youngest boy on the show didn't have anything substantial that year nor did his stand-in – who was a little person. Burt fought for everybody and demanded that we write something for Jacob and the little people. Victor looked at Brent and I and said, "Burt's your friend … you write it.".   What's the deal with me and little people? Well, at least I'm writing for them instead of blowing them.   This script had the makings of a disaster. In year one and two, Jacob was so adorable that he could score every time you went to him because he had that cute kid factor. As he grew older, he was still an exceptional young man, but the cuteness factor wore off, and it was harder to understand him because he didn't articulate well. Also, we needed to give more to Jay Ferguson and a little person.

I had an idea that Jacob was getting bullied by a little girl at school and when Burt went to confront the parents, Burt was bullied by a little person.   It was Brent and my friendly way of getting back at our boss and friend. The A story had Marilu's old friend come back in town and had a date with her son Jay Ferguson. We were lucky to get Kathie Lee Gifford to be our star! What a beautiful, real person she is. We also had John Ratzenberger, from *Cheers* direct the episode. He was so cool.

John was hilarious and shared a great story with me on how he landed his role on *Cheers*. John went in for the part of Norm … and could tell right there in the room they were going to go in a different direction.

John could have done what most actors do … say "Thank you" and leave, but John became **ASSERTIVE** and became a problem solver. Directors, producers, and writers love problem solvers.   John pitched and began playing the role of a know it all Cliff Clavin. The producers and writers loved it and created his character. That **RISK** that decision to be **ASSERTIVE** made John Ratzenberger part of television history and made him a fortune.

Burt was uncharacteristically not very supportive of John. I had no idea why.   I was not in the dressing room with him all of the time anymore, but it was just not the loving welcoming Burt that I was accustomed to seeing most of the time. There was even a moment where he tried to do one of his "friendly" slaps to John that if memory serves well broke his glasses or at minimum knocked them off his face. I saw it and was unsettled. If this was in any other work environment that could have been a terrible thing. John, fortunately, blew it off and just continued to do a great job.

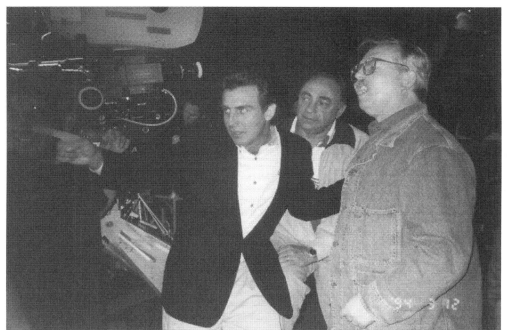
John Ratzenberger posed me in this picture to pretend I was showing him what to do ... yeah right.

John Ratzenberger directed, Kathie Lee Gifford starred, and I co-wrote the episode.

Kathie Lee Gifford went completely against type to play this role and did it incredibly well. She was every bit as nice in person as you see on TV. I remember after the episode calling her once on her show and she was so nice to pick up. Great lady!

Somehow this episode on paper that Brent and I did was nowhere near as good as the other one we wrote for Jerry Reed but as miracles happen and the bizarre world of our business works this episode turned out really good. I think even with Kathie Lee talking up our show with Regis … we were in real trouble. Burt was working hard and doing his very best to keep it alive, but if anyone was ever experienced to weather storms, it was Burt Reynolds. He cared. He cared a great deal … not only for the show but the cast and crew. He wore that on his sleeves. He felt responsible for helping everyone whatever our fate would be Burt would be okay.

Burt was resilient and always talked about getting off the mat. My dad already taught me to never quit, but Burt reinforced it, and it was neat to see Because of Burt …

... TOUGH

Burt Reynolds was a legit tough guy! My favorite football player of all-time was Jack Youngblood, and he was tough. He broke his leg and still played in the Superbowl and Burt, and I talked about Jack a lot. Burt was country tough. Much stronger than he knew. He would jokingly slap people and did it to me once and it fricken hurt. One time I asked Dom DeLuise about it, and he said it really hurt. I sincerely don't think Burt knew how strong he was.

I have a few incidents I witnessed of his toughness.

On *Evening Shade* there was a stunt where he rolled out of a moving van and at the time, he was in his late 50's. I remember every one of us was worried about him. If he gets hurt the series is done - at least for a while ... so why not get a stuntman? But Burt insisted. I was right in the van with him when he jumped out and rolled. He did it over and over and over. No problem. Now that I am in my mid 50's ... I hurt just thinking about it.

In another episode, there was a gimmick in a motor home where Michael Jeter and Burt were in the scene, and Burt was supposed to catch on fire. They put a substance on his hands and arms to protect him from burning, but he was really lit on fire. The prop master filled the fire extinguishers with baby powder instead because after all, what is safer than baby powder right? What nobody knew back then was baby powder was highly flammable. So, when Michael Jeter sprayed him with it instead of extinguishing the fire, it blew up in Burt's face in front of a live audience. It singed his eyebrows, and we feared it damaged his lungs. Burt insisted we keep shooting and the longer we argued, the worse it would get. I'm not sure if we finished the rest of the show that night but remember our team finally convinced him to go to the hospital against his will, and I was in the emergency room with Loni.

This is a funny story but TRUE! And you get the REAL story here. Before Wrestlemania 10, it was in the news that Burt Reynolds was attacked and mugged outside a bookstore. Burt beat them up, and that is why he had a cast on for Wrestlemania 10. That may or may not have been right about the fight, but that is not how he broke his hand. Here is the real story.

In the episode Brent and I wrote, Burt went to confront the bully's father and saw the little person who was a bully too. The little person pushed Burt over a couch. Burt fell to the ground and got up and quietly looked at me and casually said: "I just broke my hand."

"WHAT?!"

"I just broke my hand." I couldn't believe it, but it was true. I know he was in pain, but he finished the show and then went to go get a cast. I was with him in New York for Wrestlemania 10, and it was a blast, and the story was he broke it on some thugs faces who tried to mug him. The truth is, he broke it getting pushed over a couch by a little person. Now you tell me which story sounds better before Wrestlemania? And that's where we were going Because of Burt ...

... WRESTLEMANIA and WRESTLING

With Burt and the Macho Man Randy Savage.

When I was a kid in St. Louis my dad and I would race home from church to watch Roller Derby and Wrestling At The Chase on TV. I didn't know what I enjoyed more watching my dad make an audible grunt noise and twitch his shoulder as if he was punching along with Dick "the Bruiser" or actually watching the wrestling. Both were so enjoyable. My grade school friends and I would pretend to be wrestlers on the trampoline. Raking eyes and announcing the moves we would make on one another as we made them. In my fraternity (the Pikes) in college (University of Missouri) we would have 30 plus guys in the Chapter room watching wrestling once a week screaming and yelling at the television. One time we all surprised dates and took them to a wrestling match. At first, they were appalled and in utter disbelief that they were at a wrestling match, but by the end, they were screaming louder than we were. I did a report in a speech class at Mizzou around 1981 about the popularity and potential massive success of professional wrestling. The teacher encouraged me to change topics "because nobody cares about that stuff that my grandfather used to watch." I knew she was wrong and debated her about the carnival-like atmosphere.

Good vs. evil. All-American good guys, evil Iranian's, Russian's and Germans, red-necks, masked men, Playboys, cowboys, Indians, and of course Giants. All in all great action, great athleticism and morality tales being told through this unique circus-like entertainment. I didn't sell my teacher on it, and she had her mind made up. I needed to switch the topic. I had my mind made up too – I was going to do it because I believed in it. I did the speech on professional wrestling and received an A on my presentation and a D on my topic. Thus I got a C for the class. I was upset and apparently "wrong" in the class, but right in life.

Just four years later in 1985 was the first WrestleMania and what was once her grandfather's little dinky pastime was now a major global success. In retrospect, I would prefer to be "right" in life over "wrong" in the class. If my teacher could only see me now in writing this, I am doing the Triple H crotch chop indicating for her to you know what. ☺ I guess I had the last laugh.

When my wife and I moved to Los Angeles, we had a rare opportunity to spend way above our means to go sit in the front row to watch my favorite wrestler Ric Flair fight Hulk Hogan for the first time. Julie couldn't believe the atmosphere of the night. The crowd was crazy fun, the action intense, the referee was jawing with me and even flipped me off. All part of the act. We are not big spenders, but on that night, we spent money to see history and had a blast.

Because of Burt, I developed a relationship with an upper management person from Hasbro who was a part of the wrestling line of action figures. All I wanted to know is what wrestling figures they planned on making for the upcoming year and asked if I could see the prototypes on paper. He loved Burt and was happy to help so not only did I get to see the prototypes, but he would send me boxes of Hasbro Wrestling figures. I was so moved and grateful. I was getting stuff before it was out and none of that would have happened without Burt Reynolds.

Many stars would just come to the set of *Evening Shade* to watch the show or hang out with Burt. Because of Burt Reynolds, I was able to meet one of the most iconic wrestlers of all time … Hulk Hogan.

Burt would get gifts daily, offers to do things, tickets to various events. Burt knew I loved wrestling and when they would come to Los Angeles, he would get us tickets and backstage passes. Are you kidding me??? We would get to go backstage and meet the wrestlers??!! All Because of Burt! We had great seats, then someone would bring us backstage, and we were able to meet The Undertaker, Bret Hart, and Shawn Michaels to name a few.

With Hulk Hogan in Burt's dressing room.

Then there was WrestleMania 10 in Madison Square Garden. The WWE (then WWF) signed Burt to come to New York, and Burt asked me to go with him along with Scott Jackson. I was going with Burt Reynolds to WrestleMania? We arrived the day before and were picked up in a limo by Senior Vice President of the WWE, Ed Cohen. Ed was terrific, and there was an instant bond between Ed and us.

Ed had a limp from cancer surgery and as is Burt's motto, "everyone matters" and immediately took to Ed. He was encouraging to Ed, and I could tell it meant a lot to him. He took us to the ritzy Carlyle Hotel and in the words of Ric Flair "We were limousine riding and stylin' and profiling."

Ed called us later in the day and asked us to go to dinner, and he might have a former champion joining us. I was like a kid in a candy store jumping up and down to Burt, "Dad can we go? Can we please go"? Burt smiled with great joy when he could make others happy, and he did it for a lifetime. He encouraged me to go, but he wanted to stay in the hotel that night. I was there to serve and support Burt. I wanted to make sure he was okay with it, but he was insistent. "Go. Have a great time". Who would have guessed that WWE history would be created that night? I showed up to this incredible restaurant, and there was Ed and with him was former Champion, Bob Backlund. Bob Backlund!!! My dad and I watched him growing up on Wrestling at the Chase. Bob was a legit wrestler and a legit good guy who was the Champion for 6 years. That is a long time to hold the belt for a company, and I was having dinner with him. Ed and Bob were as interested in Hollywood stories as I was about wrestling stories.

Bob Backlund Body slamming me outside of a restaurant the night before Wrestlemania 10.

The one thing I wanted to establish right from the top was that Burt had a lot of respect for wrestlers, their athleticism, and the beating they took on a nightly basis. Wrestlers were a lot like Burt … if you treated them with respect, they would give it back tenfold, but if you pissed them off look out because all bets were off. I laid that groundwork early because, it was the truth, but also I wanted to protect Burt and make sure nobody would use him on an angle without him knowing about it. "If you want to do something Burt would probably be game, but just let us know." They had other guest stars like Little Richard, Jennie Garth, Donnie Wahlberg, but the one thing I was insistent about was they keep Sy Sperling away from Burt. I was sure Sy was a great guy, but Sy was the President for the Hair Club for Men, and I didn't want any cheap shot connection being made about Burt's hair for a cheap joke. I assured them it would not be worth it. I didn't know if that was something they were considering or not, but I felt my message was heard, respected and that would not be an issue.

With Little Richard backstage at Madison Square Garden for the event.

Throughout the night I was pinching myself thinking how fortunate I was to be in New York hanging out with the former WWE Champion and the senior vice president of the company and it was all Because of Burt. My steak was delicious, and the drinks kept coming and perhaps because of the drinks I dared to pitch an idea to them about Bob. "You were the Champion for 6 years in a row. You carried the company for all of those years. All of the hype with WrestleMania's and money that the company and wrestlers made today thanks to you … where is your respect for doing things the right way and paving the way for these guys?

I think you should come back as Bitter Bob Backlund and be psychotically pissed for not getting the credit you deserve." Bob and Ed looked at each other like "Holy crap." Bob started doing a little of it right there on the spot, and it was organic for him. Playing a bad guy was just not Bob but use the history of the years he carried the company and see the massive success of what wrestling became without honoring his tenure made sense. Where was his appreciation? That was organic. Real. That was something Bob could do, and the seeds were planted. We had a blast together, and as we said goodnight, Bob Backlund effortlessly picked me up for a body slam and gently laid me down. What a special night for me.

It's WrestleMania 10, and we were escorted backstage where all the magic was. I was used to seeing stars every day in Hollywood, but this was my childhood … and I was running into all these wrestlers that I had their mini wrestling figures at home. "Burt; this is Yokozuna, "he's the champion, Yokozuna … Burt Reynolds". "Bret and Owen Hart please meet Burt Reynolds. Burt, Bret, and Owen." Ed gave us an option to hang in the back with the wrestlers where we could watch the event on the big screen or sit in a box to watch the event. Burt wanted to hang with the wrestlers, and it was a mutual love fest. "Burt, Macho Man Randy Savage – Macho Man Burt."

Then I was able to meet the main man – Vince McMahon. He couldn't be any kinder, and I was stunned at how relaxed he was. His product that he was producing and announcing was being televised all over the world. He was as calm as could be. This was going to have two World Championship matches and an Intercontinental Championship.

Burt and I with Owen Hart

The good guys and bad guys were seemingly all one in the back. It was no different than what we did. They were great performers and athletes that were out there entertaining their butts off with one significant difference … they sometimes hurt each other. During the famous ladder match between Shawn Michaels and Razor Ramon, the room was packed with wrestlers. I learned some new terminology like "oooh there's a potato" which meant that was a real punch. In that match, there was a lot of potatoes, and it goes down as one of the best matches of all time. After that match, every one of us left the room to greet the wrestlers for their incredible match. As they came off, if memory serves me correctly, Shawn had a huge black and blue welt on his side which required him to go to the hospital with broken ribs.

Burt went out for the main event, and I watched backstage with bated breath. I prayed he would have a great experience like I had been having. I also prayed nobody would mess with him for some unseen angle, because if they did Burt would fight them. I would feel a sense of responsibility that I failed my boss and friend. Thank God Burt did his job and the WWE was thrilled with Burt and he was with them. As I said goodbye, I knew that Ed Cohen would be a lifer … a friend that I would stay in touch with and this relationship was just beginning.

Shortly after WrestleMania 10, Ed and Bob Backlund pitched the idea we discussed to Vince, and he liked it. Bob did it to perfection, and the once baby face became a real heel. The gimmick worked, and his hated popularity grew. He became the number 1 heel in the company and was so successful they gave him the Championship belt again beating the company's favorite wrestler at that time Bret Hart. Wow, again … a surreal moment from watching Wrestling at the Chase as a kid to going to WrestleMania with Burt and pitching this idea to Ed and Bob Backlund. Them using the idea shortly after that and it worked and worked great! All this Because of Burt Reynolds … but there was something even more exciting about to happen.

Vince McMahon wanted to fly me to Titan Towers to meet with him. What?? The CEO – the cool guy I met backstage – the man who took Wrestling to a whole new level was flying me out to see him. Jet flyin, limousine ridin' Mark Fauser was being escorted into Titan Towers Studio to see where a lot of their work was shot. Everyone was so kind to me including Ed Cohen who set it all up. Seeing Vince was truly inspiring. He did what I loved and wanted to hear my thoughts about his multi-billion-dollar company.

He showed me around and then took me to his house for dinner. What? I was going to Vince McMahon's house for dinner???? Burt Reynolds, I love you.

There I was at his house, and he introduced me to his wonderful wife Linda and kids Shane and Stephanie. Shane and Stephanie went back into a TV room as Vince, Linda and I sat down for three hours discussing the business. One thing Vince was adamant about was when I would say wrestling, he would correct me and say "WWF." He shared with me the overwhelming odds he faced against Ted Turner and his cable empire who owned his competitor wrestling (sorry Vince) organization WCW. Vince was a star maker and a great creator of characters (Undertaker, Ultimate Warrior, Razor Ramon, etc). He had the marketing wherewithal to take Hulk Hogan and the WWF to the promised land. He also put on a superior looking product with lighting etc.... and brilliant to brand to kids, opening up a whole financial market to figures, lunchboxes and millions and millions of dollars' worth of merchandising.

The WCW had many elements I liked though … they had more of the mystique of wrestling (sorry Vince) that I fell in love with. Their stuff seemed less scripted and more real, and to me, that was the magic of wrestling. We all knew the outcome was predetermined but were they really getting mad? That punch looked real!! The more realistic, the better. He asked me my thoughts on Jake the Snake Roberts, Lex Lugar, Mark Henry, Sunny and many of the wrestlers. I encouraged him to try to get Ric Flair back. I told him that he played it so real and his need for the championship belt was like his Viagra.

My kids with Brock Lesnar

He asked my thoughts on where I saw the business going, and I remembered saying it was historically good vs. evil or black and white which apparently worked, but I felt that the future would be the characters in the gray. The anti-heroes which added layers to a character and gave the audience something uniquely different.

I'm not sure if I was one of many to think that way, but it wasn't long after that that Stone Cold Steve Austin (one of Vince's most celebrated creations) came on the scene. The ultimate anti-hero. He was so bad he was good. Nobody would tell Stone Cold what to do. Being the ultimate team player, Vince would even let Stone Cold make him bleed, pour beer on him, give him many stunners and one time he hit Vince with a bedpan. Vince saw my passion for his business and something his wife reinforced to me was that Vince would outwork anyone. This business was with him morning noon and night. I was beyond impressed with his passion and his love for the company. His marketing was brilliant and would have a profound effect on me in future projects.

Vince and I really hit it off, and he drove me to my hotel, and that night I received a call from the human resource person that they wanted to hire me. Vince asked me to go on the road with him and Ed to observe how it all worked behind the scenes. I was so fascinated by how they would get the wrestlers in a large room to go over the outline for the evening.

I was with them for about 4 days and nights to see it all work. I liked it – but traveling every day and doing it all over was not my gig – plus I was missing my family and felt that I had more to do in Hollywood. So we said goodbye, and I was and am eternally grateful to Vince McMahon and his staff. Ed and I remained close friends from that point on. In fact, Ed invited me to WrestleMania 12 in Anaheim while I was out there. I was in the box seats above and again saw Vince and company, and they couldn't have been nicer. When the WWE would come to Indiana, Ed would always get us passes to watch the event and go backstage.

With Ric Flair and Julie and the kids.

One of Ed's last events, before he retired, was introducing me to my all-time favorite wrestler Nature Boy Ric Flair. The Naitch was so cool and kind ... "You have a beautiful family." He said, and then he signed his book for me. What a great memory. What a great experience and it was all Because of Burt.

Ed retired, and we would talk about once a year, and I knew he was delighted with his new bride. He always asked me about Burt, and I would ask him about wrestling. It is a friendship that I would forever cherish. Ed Cohen was one of the longest-tenured employees at the WWE and one of the greatest venue bookers of all-time. He tragically passed away August 25th, 2018, and I hope that he booked the best seats in heaven for him and Burt.

As we headed back to Los Angeles to finish off season four, we were about to get body slammed and respectfully speaking I don't think it was just Because of Burt …

... BODY SLAMMED

Burt continued to fight hard for the show and others. His generous heart never ceased. Burt surprised Jay Ferguson, the young teenage actor on our show by buying him a car.

He had hired Mike Henry, the former professional football player, who played Tarzan. He was second fiddle to Jackie Gleason in the *Smokey And The Bandit* films. **EVERYONE MATTERS.**

Mike was one of the politest people ever and came on the show to serve and help on the crew. He was a great looking guy, but like all good things that come to end Mike had to **REINVENT.** What I learned was Mike was dealing with early stages of Parkinson's, and Burt was loyal to help find a place for another valued friend.

The ratings were good enough to warrant us to come back, and if things in his life were calming down and that was the case, there would be no reason why we wouldn't be back. Burt told me he was told by CBS that we were coming back. Brent and I were doing better than ever at this point and with another year under our belts, it would be a difference maker. In late May we were at the office together and received a call that our show was canceled. It was devastating to all of us. For one, it was a great show and the longer it would be on the more money everybody would make in syndication. Waiting that long to tell us was hard for other people on the staff to find other work in time. Many of the people who once told Burt "yes" for everything he said, were nowhere to be found. I was worried about my family and my career, but I was really sad for the man who gave so much to so many. Where was everybody? I could tell Burt was crushed. Crushed! There is something about the business when you are up everybody loves you and wants you, but when you're down and need support the most, people leave, and I was so disheartened to see that.

I knew Burt had so much more to offer with his talent and that he was a fighter and incredibly **RESILIENT.**

Scotty Jackson, Dale Stern and I and a few others helped Burt pack up his huge home and put it in a moving truck for Jupiter Florida. While moving Burt's stuff, Dale and I uncovered nude photos of a beautiful, well-known actress never seen before. Wow! This was a prize!

This was money! My wife and I made a deal that if I couldn't find something by October, we too would leave and go back to her hometown of Marion, Indiana. May to October is not a lot of time to land a big one, but with the cost of living there and having two kids, it was what it was.

I needed money! I needed a job! "Hey, what if we took that picture and sold it to Penthouse? That would give us the money we needed to stay in the game, and that would buy us plenty of time out there to live and find something else. Who would know it was us? Everyone else does it why shouldn't we? Right is Right and wrong is - oh screw it with the morality crap Fauser!
You're a sinner too! You need the money!" said the devil on my shoulder. Wait a minute!!!! What the hell was wrong with us? We were now becoming the MONSTER we hate! That is the normalization when everyone else does it why can't we syndrome. I was ashamed of myself for even having those thoughts. Burt trusted us to move his stuff, and we needed to honor him! It was not fair to the actress to expose her for our gain, and it was not our character to do that. It just wasn't worth it, and I am glad we didn't, but the fact that we even thought about it for a day was a sign for me that I needed to leave and get a dose of integrity and reality again.

Fran Bascom, a casting agent for *Evening Shade*, was working for a soap opera and landed a role for me with the potential to keep us out there. I was so excited. There was hope. I was asked to go in to get fitted for costumes and was getting pumped. Suddenly, I received the most apologetic call from Fran who regretfully informed me that my role was being completely changed to a black woman. Well, there's nothing I can do about that. That was probably another sign for me to leave and the decision was made.

The Fauser's were sadly leaving Los Angeles. With three weeks to go, a fellow writer friend of mine from *Evening Shade*, Susan Wick, was working for a TV show called *Model's Inc*. She was able to get me an audition which I landed and shot. It went well, and Aaron Spelling asked Susan about me and wanted to bring me back. Incredible. This could be the gig to get me back into the game. I showed up on the set to play my role again and guess who was directing? The same crappy director I had on the reshoot of *Seaquest*.

Of all of the directors out there how on earth did I get the same no talent guy? We did the scene in practice, and then he moved the camera behind my back to sabotage me. He was doing it again!!! Instead of getting a master shot of both of us which was the standard thing to do followed up with close-ups for coverage he was going to squash me. My mind started racing. What do I do? I need this job and don't want to go to Marion. Nor did I know what I would do there. Somebody help me!!! All of a sudden, I heard "Action," and I couldn't say any of my lines. The d-bag director audibly was disgusted, and I was in a complete fog. "Action!" Again, nothing and the director "What the hell!!".

I wanted to punch him, but there were too many people around. I wanted to leave – watching all of these extras in the scene looking at me like "I could do it," "Let me do it." Frankly, I wanted them to do it. I wanted to get out of there because I knew, either way, I was buried. We did it again, and I was able to get through the scene and as I expected the back of my head would be featured in the next episode. I went after the director afterward and had several people escort me away. I felt good about telling that no talent, off and it was so worth it. That, however, was the worst, most embarrassing acting experience I ever had in my life. Time was running out.

I then received a call from my friends from the TV show *Coach*. Patrick Sean Clark, my writer-actor buddy from Mizzou, was on the same softball team with me, Tony Dow (Wally from *Leave it To Beaver*) who was directing the episode, and actor Bill Fagerbakke who was one of the stars on the show.

I was getting work at the eleventh hour and was wondering if this was the devil tempting me to stay or an angel? The *Coach* episode was the last week I was in town. Friday night we would tape the show and Saturday I would start my journey back to the Midwest.

Jerry VanDyke, one of the stars from *Coach*, had an Uncle in Marion Indiana and was very familiar with that city and had nothing but nice things to say. Julie and the kids had already left. I was shooting my final episode of anything and possibly forever on Friday night in October. On the set of Universal Studios on that Friday, I received a call … and again things would change in large part Because of Burt …

... THE RIGHT TO REMAIN SILENT

I received a call about selling our first movie *The Right To Remain Silent*.

The Right To Remain Silent started as a monologue in Charles Nelson Reilly's acting class in LA.

When many of us graduated BRIT and went to Los Angeles, I begged Charles to let me help him open a school so we can stay sharp in our craft.

In 1991, we created the Faculty in North Hollywood, where Charles would often play Ruth Draper tapes and encourage us to write and create our own characters as she did. So many of us started writing.

Lisa Soland wrote scenes in class that turned into plays, and today she is a prolific playwright. Others wrote as well. Brent and I had an idea about doing a series of monologues about social issues and why various people were getting arrested on a given evening. They had *The Right To Remain Silent* but couldn't help themselves and shared their stories.

This gave us an opportunity to write about topics and things we were trying to figure out in life too. It's important to write what you know ... so my first attempt, I wrote a semi-true story about what happened to me in college. One night, my Pike buddies and I were driving home from the famous Thursday night bar scene at Mizzou. We lived in A-Frame apartments off in the woods.

A police officer pulled me over and came up to my window and said, "Do you know you were driving in the middle of the road"? I confidently said

"Yes." He looked at me incredulously and asked why and I said, "to protect the animals." My friends started to laugh and went into the quick shop knowing I was in big trouble. The officer looked at me like this ought to be interesting ... but it was 100 percent true. "Out here animals come running out on the road, and if I drive in the middle of the road I have more time to react, and I could see better perfuly ... perif ..." Of course, I couldn't say the word peripherally. The police officer asked if I was

Charles sent me this picture of Ruth Draper and my quote in a frame that I have in my office.

drinking and I said "yes." Again, he couldn't believe my blunt honesty, but I was respectful, truthful and knew I didn't drink that much, so I was trying to make light out of the extremely stressful situation. He asked me to get out of the car and gave me a sobriety test. He was professional to me and knew I was harmless but had a job to do and I was doing really well until we got to the alphabet.

"A,b,c,d,e,f,g,h, i,j,k,l,m,n,o,z," He said, "Mr. Fauser do you know your alphabet?"

"Yes, but I have to sing it. That's how I learned the alphabet by singing it not saying it. Who the hell can just say it?!! So, I sang it, and the officer laughed and let me go. Thank God.

So, you write what you know, and I thought what if I play this likable, successful businessman with the whole world ahead of him with a twist?

I could make people laugh, and suddenly we learn at the same time he does, that he made a tragic mistake, blacked out and accidentally killed someone?   My writing could give me tools as an actor to show a wide range of emotions to play: from funny, to perturb, to angry, too shocked, to emotionally devastated. When you write your own stuff, you stand to get criticized not only on the writing but the acting. But, if you succeed, you could score on both, and that is the risk you take. That is what could set you apart from the rest. I did the monologue in class and Charles flipped. He was so excited and talked about it over and over in class! Charles called me at home later that night, and that was always a good sign.

At the time, before Evening Shade, Brent was struggling and working at Domino's Pizza.   While delivering pizzas, he was robbed at gunpoint, and they also would get pizzas out of the deal. Brent was so funny and yet angry about his experience.   He did a great monologue about the dangers of being a pizza delivery person. All of this writing was unique and different and couldn't be compared to the million times Charles had to sit through an agonizing scene from *Agnes of God*.   Charles went on and on about Brent and my piece in class and then called Burt and told him with great enthusiasm like only Charles could do "You should see their play - it's WONDERFUL." Burt called me the next day which was around May of 1992, at his office where I worked for him and said, "Hey guy, Charles told me about your play, and I would like you to do it at my theater."

"Oh my God, I would be honored. Thank you. When do you want to do it?"

"Next week."

There was a moment's pause of sheer terror - does he know we only have 2 monologues written?

How can we write a whole play in a week? Forget that how can we do an established play in a week??? This is crazy?? This is insane"! Those were all my thoughts and many more negative things racing through my head in a millisecond. I quickly said, "Great. Thank you so much." We hung up the phone, and I said to myself what have I done?

We can't do this! Wait! The hell we can't. **<u>SEIZE THE OPPORTUNITY</u>**

We were trained to find a way to make things work, so it was on. We were going to do it.

I called Brent, and he went off the charts nuts. "What the F*ck! Are you f*ckin' crazy?! You son of a bitch - we can't do this! Does he know it ain't written?"

"NO, I didn't tell him that!!! Brent, we can do this! They are booking our flights as we speak. Burt's flying us down and putting us up and everything."

Honestly, Brent was the most motivated I had ever seen him in my life. He wanted to get out of delivering pizzas, and this could be his chance to get out of it ... so he agreed. Our friend Dale Stern who is now an Emmy award-winning director and a great guy ... worked in the office with me and could hear Brent screaming in panic. Being the prankster that Dale was, he called Brent as the "driver," and told him the flight was moved up several hours, and we were leaving today. Brent started screaming and told him he's doing the best he could to pack.

Then Dale called him again as the "driver" and said the car was outside his apartment because Burt pushed up the flight. Brent went ballistic and said a record number of F-bombs. The country twang of his cussing was classic.

We started laughing and told him that it was all BS, but we did have to get packed and go. Back then we had FAX Machines, so we started writing like crazy and then sending faxes down to the cast in Florida. With Burt's apprentices, I knew we were in good hands because of their training and work ethic. I knew they would give us everything they had to help us create this do or die situation.

That week we were directing the actors and writing other monologues for the cast and ourselves because Brent and I were going to play 2 parts each. 1 WEEK! 1 WEEK to pull off a miracle Because of Burt. We pulled all-nighters and were running on full adrenaline. One could have easily made excuses and postponed it, but the opportunity might not have ever come again.

We were writing about drunk driving, AIDS, homelessness, abortion, racism, euthanasia, cross-dressing, death penalty, etc.... and we went at these topics with passion, humor, heart and many thought-provoking twists and turns. Brent and I did everything in our powers to get the cast ready and spent very little time on our own pieces.

Brent played two roles that were beyond brilliant. One was an elderly lady with kids who got into a fight at Kmart over a dress. Brent's days of doing *Greater Tuna* for Jaston Williams and Joe Sears really served him well here. He was hysterical and brought the house down. It was well needed comic relief following my monologue of an elderly man who struggled to euthanize his beloved wife to honor her wishes. The play is a real roller coaster ride of emotions.

In Act II, I played a guy who thought he was Captain Kirk and was arrested at a Star Trek convention for fighting a Klingon. He was trying to warn the planet about the importance of resolving race issues. Hilarious stuff and yet incredibly poignant. Brent played a homeless man with smart dialogue and funny moments who at the end we learned he was obsessed about getting his refrigerator box back to house his pregnant wife. We tested two pieces in class, but the rest of this would all have to be a massive leap of faith. What if the ultra-conservative crowd down there were appalled by some of the topics and language? I remember being at lunch at Schooners the afternoon of the performance with my mother-in-law Nancy Harris, Aunt Connie Harris, Hanne, and Bill Morrison. I thought I was going to get sick and it wasn't because of the blackened dolphin I ate, it was because of the overwhelming pressure.

It was merely a God thing. It was so out of our hands, and we just had to hope that the talented cast would come through and the audience would get it. Everyone hit it out of the park, and the audience was incredible. It was a real miracle! The original play can be seen on YouTube.

The reports came back to Burt and Charles that the play went over tremendously and their investment in us paid off.

He gave his players the ball, and we scored. My father in law James Harris bought a bunch of party supplies afterward for us to party at Burt's condo's where we were staying, and it was utterly surreal. This huge condo is where the stars would visit when we were apprentices, and now Brent and I were there in Burt's condo stylin' and profilin' with these talented apprentices.

SEIZE THE OPPORTUNITY, **WORK** hard and take a leap of **FAITH** is the lesson I always try to pass down to young artists. What would have happened if we had not done those things? Life is about choices … seize the opportunity when it comes.

In early 1993, The Right To Remain Silent was performed in Los Angeles at the Tamarind Theater by many of our talented apprentice friends from various classes. They were so good. Burt brought Loni, and many of the cast members from *Evening Shade* and several other stars out to see it including higher-ups at Showtime.

Burt and Loni with Brent and I and several of our remarkable cast members from the "Right To Remain Silent" in Los Angeles.

God bless Burt Reynolds. Showtime liked it and liked it a lot! They told me that night how much they liked it and wanted to do it!

They called me the next day to tell me how much they liked it! We went out to lunch and talked about it. They wanted to make this movie, and that was all Because of Burt.

In 1994, some time had passed, and the highly public and toxic divorce of Burt and Loni combined by the demise of our successful TV show, caused Showtime to get distant from the project. I couldn't understand it. What does that have to do with me?

I saw their reaction to the play just a year ago! I talked to them many times and heard their enthusiasm. How was it that they didn't believe in the project anymore? The project was dead!!

Around June of 1994, my awesome sister in Law, Jodi Harris, and her wonderful partner Lynn Howarth, found a way to make it happen from Colorado. Yes, Colorado!

Lynn took care of horses for a producer in Colorado named Debbie Robbins. Imagine that? Not Los Angeles where I was on a major studio, surrounded by stars and executives, but a horse farm in Colorado from a family connection.

Debbie Robbins was working with Donna Dubrow who was married to a powerhouse A-list director, John McTiernan (from *Die Hard* fame) and Debbie's husband was Hubert De La Bouillerie, an editor who was looking to make his directorial debut.

They wanted to make a movie I wrote called *Home Field Advantage* (which was optioned before). It was the football version of *Field of Dreams*. A real feel-good movie. Hubert loved it and was a very visual person who was extremely passionate which I liked.

I did another pass on the script to incorporate the ideas we discussed, and Hubert and the producers went to Disney to pitch it. They left and called me right away and felt it was going to happen. I was so stoked because I would need something now that *Evening Shade* and *Seaquest* were done and the clock was ticking, or we were going to leave LA.

The following week we found out it was not going to happen!!! So depressing. Now what? I threw a Hail Mary and pitched them *The Right To Remain Silent* and shared with them Showtimes thoughts. They loved it. Jana Sue Memel became part of the team and was the executive producer.

Showtime was interested again and loved it. Wow, this was so confusing to me, but the lesson I eventually learned from all of this was that it was often not about the script or the writer, but it was about who was hot, who was attached and what star was shining. Hollywood bets on the **WAVE** that is going up and runs away from the wave that is going to crash.

I kept trying to explain to the producers and Showtime how great Burt was. How lucky I was to have Burt in my life and without him, this would have never happened … which was factually true … but they didn't want him, and that was that. It hurt me because I wanted to give back to the man who gave me so much. His acting was so underrated from things I witnessed in class and in person, but this project wouldn't be it.

On the set of Universal Studios on Friday night doing the show *Coach* the night before I moved to Indiana, I received a call from Debbie Robbins telling me they sold *The Right To Remain Silent*. YES! Talk about clutch timing, but at the time I was already committed to leaving. The next day the guys were going to help me pack, and I was going to take my long trek back to Indiana.

The movie would have to be far more visual than the play and whatever we could show instead of saying we would. Hubert was very good at that, and he helped us develop an excellent script based on the play we did. I co-wrote the screenplay from Marion, Indiana while Brent was in Moberly Missouri. They liked the screenplay, and we were greenlit to make it.

Fortunately, they started landing great actors in the roles we wrote. Like the drunk driver, I wrote from my experience at Mizzou was going to be played by the handsomely talented Patrick Dempsey.

The elderly man I wrote and played in Jupiter in the original production was now being performed by the legendary Carl Reiner.

The homeless piece that Brent did so brilliantly was being played by the iconic Christopher Lloyd.

The Pizza person Brent wrote based on his own experience would be played by Amanda Plummer.

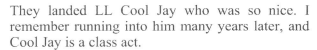

They landed LL Cool Jay who was so nice. I remember running into him many years later, and Cool Jay is a class act.

Judge Reinhold was cast. Judge was one of the first apprentices at Burt's place, and we reminisced about it later at Burt's funeral.

Laura San Giacomo and Fisher Stevens also joined the team.

Our two leads were fellow Mizzou graduate Robert Loggia and the talented and attractive Leah Thompson. It was an incredible cast and was beyond moved that they would do it.

The trailer was great, but the Movie I felt lacked the comedy of the play which was important to offset some of the heavy topics and have the full range of emotions that was needed. Needless to say ... I was so honored that we had that cast and made the film. There were moments that I pictured precisely in my head as a writer that was captured forever on film and what an incredible feeling.

Cable TV review
'Right to Remain Silent'

By Laurence Vittes

Tucked away into Sunday night, "The Right to Remain Silent" is an intriguing, slightly offbeat example of the all-star anthology genre marking the directorial debut of Hubert de la Bouillerie. The pacing is deceptively effective in a minimalist way, and while some of the star turns are flat, the whole is impressively more than the sum of the parts.

Framed by a rookie cop's first night as a booking officer in a big city police station, "Right" tells the stories of an African-American filmmaker (LL Cool J) who infiltrated the Klan; a drunken driver (Patrick Dempsey) who causes a fatal accident; a pistol-packing pizza delivery woman (Amanda Plummer); a husband (Carl Reiner) who helped his dying wife commit suicide; a raving husband obsessed with the talk-show host (both played by Judge Reinhold) who has influenced his newly liberated wife (Colleen Camp), a young schoolteacher (Laura San Giacomo) violently furious with her AIDs; a cross-dresser (Fisher Stevens) arrested for shoplifting; and a homeless man (Christopher Lloyd) whose profound concern

Robert Loggia and Lea Thompson are members of the ensemble cast of "The Right to Remain Silent."

for humanity is movingly displaced from his own sense of reality.

Writers Brent Briscoe and Mark Fauser have put together a coherent framework based on their own play featuring excellent dialogue that brings the best out of those actors who seem to make a personal connection with the characters they are playing, all of

See "SILENT" on page 20

'Silent'

Continued from page 16—

whom are helplessly vulnerable in a pitiless society.

Laura San Giacomo delivers a magnificent mixture of desperation and terror; Plummer takes the idiosyncrasies of her part and catches the viewers' eye and ear; and Reiner quietly screams with the pain of his loss.

None of the performances, however, is negligible and even LL Cool J continues to show that he knows what can be achieved with good acting.

Finally, Thompson and Loggia make the perfect pair to put the stories in perspective, she initially a blank slate and he so rich

THE RIGHT TO REMAIN SILENT
Showtime

Chanticleer Films, Tongue River Prods.
Executive producers .... Jana Sue Memel, John McTiernan
Producers .... Thom Colwell, Donna Dubrow, Debbie Robins
Co-producer .... Michael Fischer
Associate producer .... Hillary Anne Ripps
Director .... Hubert de la Bouillerie
Writers .... Brent Briscoe, Mark Fauser
Editor .... Michael Murphy
Director of photography .... Greg Gardiner
Music .... Randy Miller
Production designer .... Stephen Greenberg
Cast: Lea Thompson, Robert Loggia, Larry Joshua, Joyce Sylvester, Mary Pat Gleason, Geoffrey Rivas, Christopher Lloyd, Patrick Dempsey, Carl Reiner, Judge Reinhold, Amanda Plummer, Fisher Stevens, Laura San Giacomo, LL Cool J, Colleen Camp

Airdate: Sunday, Jan. 7, 10:30 p.m.-12:20

with experience, while the device of her taking mug shots is an ingenious way of allowing the viewers to gauge their own insight.

A year after it aired on Showtime, I was washing cars at my father-in-law's car dealership in Marion, fighting terrible depression of where my career went. Brent was wondering the same thing working at a liquor store in Moberly Missouri. I came home at night and turned on the television and saw people in tuxedoes and formal dresses for the Cable Ace Awards. Our movie was nominated for two Best Supporting Actress roles; Laura San Giacomo and Amanda Plummer. As I sat there filthy dirty in my work clothes, I heard them announce Amanda Plummer as the winner. She won! We won!

Our movie won, and none of this would have happened without Burt Reynolds, but instead of jumping up and down I remember tears were pouring down my cheek. That was the first time my wife saw me cry. We won and yet I felt like such a failure. Burt trained us for the ups and downs, but this was getting too tough to handle. How did he manage this all these years? The highs I experienced were better than any drug I could ever take, but the lows were devastatingly rough.

Hollywood success was just around the corner. In fact, very successful, but I am now going to jump to 2003 in Marion, Indiana to finish off *The Right To Remain Silent* Chapter.

I was now financially successful working in Hollywood, acting and writing for studio pictures, while living in Marion.

Although I coached my kid's little league teams, I felt if I was going to live in this community, I better do something to give back and do my part to help make this a better place to live. Several times my friend Marla Keppler asked me to serve on the Marion Community School of the Arts board and I was also asked to help the Civic theater. I volunteered to direct *The Right To Remain Silent* in Marion and wave our writing fees and just do it for free to help raise money for the Civic Theater. Carla Tucker who was also with the Community School of the Arts encouraged me to do it to get my feet wet. There were lots of local articles about me and my success in Los Angeles, and I could tell there was a real fascination with that from my community. I knew the town had talent because I saw it with the dance recitals from my kids … and the adults were talented too. So, I agreed to do it. I was thinking the auditions for this show were going to be wrapped around the theater.

I showed up, and Carla Tucker was the only one there to audition. How humbling! How miserably hysterical. It was fricken *Waiting For Guffman*. I asked her what we are going to do and she shrugged her shoulders "we'll figure it out." I left in defeat. A part of me wanted to see the play again to make sure my instrument was still working. The success of the published play could really get some legs and be performed all over the country since the movie was out, but I didn't need this headache. Afterward, I was at my favorite watering hole, The Mill Restaurant, drowning my miseries as I pounded down Coors Lights where my friend and owner of the bar, Geoff Eltzroth was trying to convince me not to give up on the town. "Where am I going to find an African American to play LL Cool Jay's part, a Klan member in disguise, who says, Death to all the wetbacks, dykes, kykes, chinks, spics, spades, gooks queers, … and that isn't the worst of it?". Geoff laughed and said let me ask my cook, and the cook came up from the kitchen.

Jermain McGruder was his name, and I explained to him what was up, and he would be a guy to infiltrate the Klan. He told me he never acted before but would be willing to try.

It was kind of crowded at the bar, and I thought it would be entirely inappropriate for him to be saying all of these vile things from the script out of context at the crowded bar, so I asked him to go to my car and read it. He looked at Geoff and Geoff said: "Do it!". We went to the car and Jermaine was great, and he was in. Two actors down and many more to go.

For me to do this play in Marion, Indiana I would have to be like Burt Reynolds in *The Longest Yard* and hand pick my misfit players to build a team … it was not going to be handed to me. We assembled the team and performed to sold-out houses and made the Civic theater a lot of money. Maybe because we had more time to do it, but the cast was brilliant, and this version of the show was the best I had seen. The audience and friends in my community were so kind and appreciative it inspired me to get involved and later help build the Community School of the Arts Because of Burt.

The Right To Remain Silent was later done by my alma mater, The University of Missouri, and they took it to New York where I joined them.

The play has been done throughout the country and lives on. It was also done at The Community School of the Arts with some of my incredibly talented kids and was directed by my friend Marsha Vermilion. Another terrific production. Kids contact me often about winning awards from doing the monologues, and it sure makes me feel good that others are thriving from our work. This one story about a monologue in a class that turned into a play within a week that was made into a movie with an All-Star cast won a Cable Ace Award, and was now a published play all happened Because of Burt …

... IT'S ALL ABOUT YOU

It's All About You is a filthy morality tale that was loosely based on my experience of Fame. Careful what you wish for it may come true. This started as a scene in Charles Nelson Reilly's class too. Remember you write what you know. After my bizarre encounter with my friends Michael Deal and Patrick Hughes on the movie when they called the "he a she" and all the gender confusion for me, I was motivated to write a scene about it. My fellow Burt Reynolds apprentices did this for me in class, and it was hit. I told Charles the idea came from his significant other Patrick, and he screamed with laughter.

When I was in a public bathroom with Burt, and the crazed fan was so excited he wouldn't let Burt go to the bathroom became a scene. It was a hit too. We then did it in a showcase for an audience and received huge laughs.

My time in Los Angeles and Hollywood was changing my voice as a writer. I was becoming extraordinarily cynical and mocking of the unstable world I

was around, and it clearly resonated with my peers and others. I directed two one-acts at the Tamarind theater. Because of its success, my friend Tom Kendall, who owned the theater at the time, talked about doing *It's All About You* with different casts every Friday night after the show.

Every actor would bring a different take to a character, and it was so fun, creative and different for every show we did. It was a great way to exercise our acting skills in front of a live audience that stars would come to and get a good laugh. It ran for a year, and I was so impressed with the creative, talented and diversified cast I decided to take what was a One Act and turn it into a full-length screenplay.

The OJ Simpson trial was a literal circus, the daily Jerry Springer-like talk shows that we all watched like a train wreck we mocked. This was not the journey we thought it would be. Up is down and down is up, right is wrong, and wrong is right, the world as we knew it was literally going down the toilet. If we poked fun at it, maybe others in the world would laugh along with us and share our point of view.

I wrote it from Marion, Indiana and then flew out to Los Angeles for some other pitches and together with our Burt Reynolds apprentice team of great actors we read it. We might have had about thirty people in the room all drinking and laughing hard throughout the reading. By the time we were done, fellow Burt Reynolds apprentice and dear friend, Kim Chase said, "We're going to make this movie." And by God she did it. Kim played the agent flawlessly during the show and was just amazing, but in addition to that role, she was going to produce this with her at the time husband, Robert Jacobs. She nor Robert had ever produced a movie before. I had never directed a movie before. The one thing I know now that I didn't back then is with a small budget you have to have limited sets and cast members to make it more financially viable.

Of course, my script had tons of sets and a huge cast. What the hell were we thinking? I was going to write, act and direct and now we had to pull every favor known to man to get this thing done. It was low low low budget.

Every actor we asked to do it would be doing us a huge favor, and we were so blessed to get a ton of terrific actors.

Dom DeLuise, his son Peter, Michael and their mom Carol were all in it. It was a real family affair. My next-door neighbor – Emmy and Tony Award winner Robert Morse said yes. Joel Murray, my buddy, would play a talkative cab driver that improvised the entire thing. There was a great story where he was driving in the cab, and we were in front shooting him. We were pulled over by the police and didn't have a permit to shoot. Oops! We were so low budget we couldn't afford it, and we were in big trouble. In front of us was another car pulled over by another police.

Our police officer came up to us and told us we were lucky because the guys in front of us had just stolen that car, so he let us go. Never was I so happy to see a car stolen in my life. Kim was able to get Academy Award-nominated Sally Kirkland to be kind enough to play herself.

We had a large stable of phenomenal actors from Burt Reynolds. Every one of them was/is amazingly talented. Beyond blessed that we could get our friends, these great people with a work ethic second to none. They were willing to play hard with us for 18 days and thanks to them, Kim and Robert we were able to do it.

They were all selfless friends working as production people, Ad's, making food, being extras, doing hair, whatever it took to help this small low budget movie look more significant than it was. Everyone involved was stars in my book, and my love for all of them will be everlasting.

John D'Aquino was our lead movie star, but we needed a great actress to play his girlfriend. We needed someone attractive, who could be funny, and at the eleventh hour, we were able to get former Burt Reynolds apprentice Gigi Rice. Gigi had just finished playing Will Ferrell's girlfriend in *Night At The Roxbury* and had a baby. For her and others it would be a tremendous sacrifice of time and talent.

The first night was a doozy. We were in downtown Los Angeles starting at 12:00 at night on the exterior of a movie theater. Our extras were great actors who were kind enough to play extras for the cause. I was in awe. Brent Sexton was one of Burt's apprentices and played a non-speaking security guard that night for me. Brent has since had his own television series, that is how selfless he and the rest of the Burt gang was. I just can't praise all of these talented people enough.

Kim found a studio that had virtually every one of our set pieces already built. Things were going really well. One day we shot 72 camera setups in one day. On another day we did 11 pages in one take on s steady-cam. El Nino weather threatened to bury us one day, and we had no backup plan, but God was looking out for us and gave us beautiful weather. We did run into a few fun hiccups.

Our friend Michael Deal was working as a set designer on the *Ellen Show* and thanks to him we were able to get all free set pieces for one flat fee.

Michael was in a rather serious relationship with Ron Palillo, the actor who created the memorable role of Arnold Horshack from *Welcome Back Kotter*. Ron wanted to be in the movie, and I was honored and thrilled. I created a character for him to be a sleazy tabloid guy, who could be throughout the film but had a juicy scene with Gigi Rice. This could be great for Ron to be rediscovered and great for all of us. He had the script for about two months and told me often he was so excited. Ron showed up that day and didn't know one of his lines. Not one. I asked him to just look at the script and read it as quickly as he could – it just wasn't happening. Dang it, Ron. I was such a fan of you growing up, and you need this, and so do we … why didn't you do the **WORK?** We were in trouble. Big trouble. We couldn't afford to shoot endless film watching him struggle to say one line at a time. But we couldn't afford to piss off his boyfriend either, who was our friend too because we would stop getting all of the free furniture. This just sucked. I pulled Kim and our wonderful DP Andres Garreton aside and looked for recommendations knowing he could not do it. Kim was willing to just blow the money and try to shoot him. Then we would ask a great actor who was helping us on the crew, James Smith, to go study the part and learn it, and we would shoot him later. Andres said, "We will shoot Ron, but without film." Kim and I looked at him as if to say, "Are you insane?" Andres was dead serious. We would have a small team of people that would pretend to shoot him, save money on film, get him off the set and then shoot it for real with Gigi and James Smith.

Kim and I started laughing so hard because everything about this was so wrong and yet we couldn't afford to waste the film and spend that kind of money on such a low budget movie.

It took a while for us to gain our composure and then out of respect for Gigi we shared with her our thoughts and asked her opinion, and she was like … "Hell yeah!" So we started to pretend to shoot Ron, and only a few knew of it. Gigi, the camera crew and sound man and that was it.

Peter DeLuise, who was a Godsend to me, and a knowledgeable advisor came to the set and noticed that the monitors weren't flickering and knew we weren't filming. With great urgency, he brought it to my attention, so I had to tell him. Then the Ad's found out, then everyone started to understand, and it was just a comedy within a comedy.

Once Ron left, James stepped up and did it the way it was supposed to be done, and he and Gigi killed it.

Working with Don was such an honor. He played my dad in real life and was brilliant. It was so cathartic for me to watch and meaningful how Burt tied us all together.

Dom DeLuise giving me some love.

There was a scene where we needed to shoot 7 pages in a day (which is a lot), but we had a page with a lion. Yes, a real lion. Kim was trying to convince me to use a mountain lion which would have been cheaper. In retrospect with the absurdity of the movie, it might have worked, but I was dead set on the lion because we were doing a spoof on "Tarzan Today." Kim was able to get us a lion but a young, inexperienced cheap lion.

Randy Miller was the famed, animal trainer who was there and told everyone of the danger and wanted the set cleared. Any woman who was on her period had to get out of there. We shot a lot of B-roll stuff that we needed the lion to do, and it was taking up a more significant part of the day than I hoped. Our one-page scene with John, me and the lion was up, and the trainers didn't like the way John's character looked, so they had their trainer wear his costume for rehearsals.

John D'Aquino & Gigi Rice, almost everyone in this movie, was Burt's kids.

The gig was, my character was the director and was supposed to introduce John to the seemingly harmless lion. The lion was supposed to roar, hence foreshadowing John's character imminent danger. I laid out the scene and wanted the trainer to bring the lion to me, and I was going to make the introduction.

Randy gave me a note … if something happens, don't make any quick moves or the lion will attack you. I was arrogantly like, "Great safety tip, thanks, Randy. Let's do this … and action!" Suddenly, the lion runs towards me and starts growling at me. There were no trainers around holding him as I asked. I am basically pissing in my pants while this lion is inches away from me growling in a highly agitated way. I knew something was terribly wrong because all of the trainers were screaming at the lion. I wanted to bolt but remembered I needed to hold my ground and not make any sudden moves. Terrified, I began to audibly say, "Put the lion back in the cage." "Put the lion back in the cage." Thank God, they put the lion back in the cage.

I remember how cool it was that Burt would direct himself in movies like *The End* and how he did it on *Evening Shade*. One of the advantages of directing yourself is that it's one less person you have to deal with because I knew what I wanted. One of the disadvantages is that time starts to catch up to you with all of the responsibilities, needs and wants and the planning.

Me and the hilarious Suzanne McKenney

My biggest mistake in the execution of this movie was the subject matter was too big in scope to not include hundreds and hundreds of extra's. The more significant number of people around the world that sees the rise and fall of stardom the better it would have been. That was my fault.

All in all, I couldn't have been prouder of the movie, Kim and Robert, the entire cast and crew. None of it wouldn't have happened without Burt. Virtually, the whole cast was Burt Reynolds people.

The movie was a herculean effort that when it was all said and done won the Best Comedy at the Beverly Hills Film Festival in 2001 and appeared in other festivals.

Directing John D'Aquino. We came far from our days at Burt's, but we are still near toilets.

Part of our fabulous cast from *It's All About You*.

I have written and directed many things on stage and screen before, but no other movie or project had what was in my head come to fruition like this movie in so many moments. I pop it in once a year to watch it, and to me, the story is more relevant today than it was then. Every year I laugh and admire the people and stories within the movie. I remember before the festivals I took it to Burt's house, and he and I had a private screening. He was so proud to see so many of his kids working together and of course the familiar faces like Dom, the DeLuise bunch and Robert Morse. He would give me great notes that I would address to make the movie better. It was so rewarding and my favorite project with lifelong friends that I love and am forever indebted to that I met Because of Burt …

... CITIZEN RUTH

Burt called me to go with him to Omaha Nebraska to shoot a smart comedy written and directed by the very talented Alexander Payne. Burt played a sleazy pastor and worked on his lines with me a lot. He was far more focused than I had seen in a while. It was the old Burt again, and man did we have a lot of fun together during our time there.

Do you think Burt and I had a good time? That's a big YES!

The secret in working with Burt, was if you gave him respect he would give it back tenfold, but if you disrespected him, it could get ugly. Surprisingly, some people in the industry view actors as a piece of meat and don't respect the struggle, the sacrifice, the sensitivity, and don't create a safe world for actors to pour out their emotions for all to see. Notably, some great visual directors struggle with this. They know a ton about imagery which is so important but haven't worked with actors. Their disrespectful behavior could break down the most talented actor and create a horrible working environment. I began to understand the importance of why Burt drew a respectful line throughout the years. This was not an issue here. Alexander Payne had an excellent command of the camera and worked great with actors.

This was a fun cast and would party upstairs in the hotel lounge after a busy day. Laura Dern was the lead, a terrific actress, who is just so sincere and kind. Everyone on the set loved her, and there was great history with Burt and Laura. Burt and her mom Diane Ladd and Burt and her dad Bruce Dern.

Dancing with Kelly Preston

Kelly Preston was in this movie, and she is John Travolta's wife! If only Travolta knew how he helped me during my time at Parkway Central High School in St. Louis. John Travolta had *Welcome Back Kotter*, *Saturday Night Fever* and *Grease*. I was lucky to be able to imitate Travolta really well. In fact, I was so shy to ask girls out, that I would ask them out like Vinny Barbarino or Danny Zuko. What a nerd.

As soon as I was me, it was so much harder, and that was the beauty of acting, that I could hide behind someone or something braver than me. I shared this with Kelly, and she laughed. She was so pretty, so much fun and when Grease Lighting played, she and I did Grease Lighting on the dance floor in honor of her husband.

Burt and I had many good times on this movie. One morning, we were in the lobby of the hotel getting ready to go to work, and an incredibly enthusiastic mother around Burt's age or older expressed what a huge fan she was. She shared with him that her daughter was beautiful and even a bigger fan. She showed Burt and me a picture of her daughter, and she was gorgeous! The mom said, her daughter had told everyone that although she was married, her one "gimme" in life would be if she could be with Burt Reynolds.

Burt embarrassed, smiled and laughed it off and was ready to go to work. The mom desperately said, "If I can get her to fly out here would you meet with her?" Burt was polite but noncommittal. We had to go to work, and there was a part of both of us that wondered what kind of mom would encourage her daughter to leave her husband, spend crazy money to fly to another state on a whim so she could meet Burt Reynolds. Anyway, we went to work, were gone all day and when we came back to the hotel later that evening, there was the mother with her daughter sitting in the lobby waiting for us.

The mom was right …. She was beautiful. Burt was gracious and kind and invited them up to his room. He had a huge suite, with a foyer, a living area, separated by the bedroom. He had to make an important phone call from his bedroom, and the phone call was going on longer than any of us suspected, so he gave me a signal. I thought it meant for me to tell them to leave, so I politely did, and as they went around the living area into the foyer to go … Burt hung up the phone and said "where did she go I wanted to … (I will let you figure out what he said) … just then we heard the door close. Which meant she and her mom listened to that. Like a little boy who knew he was in trouble Burt covered his mouth. I apologized because I thought he gave me the signal to have them go. He brushed it off as if it was no big deal. We went upstairs to the lounge, and there they were … the mom feeding Burt her daughter on a platter like a piece of meat. Burt was single at the time and had every right to do as he chose. To think what that mom did to her daughter was hard for me as a father to fathom doing that to any of my kids.

With Diane Ladd from *Citizen Ruth* who would later option a movie I wrote.

I knew his next job would be *Striptease* with Demi Moore, and again if I were single and available to work it would have been a blast to be on location with him. Especially to be his stand-in with the beautiful Demi Moore. I had a blast with Burt … ALWAYS. His principal photography was done. Therefore, my job was done, and although we had a few days left together and were invited to Kelly Preston's house for a party, I asked if I could go early to get back home to my wife and kids. He was bummed, and I felt like I let him down as a friend to hang with for a split second, but Burt loved my wife and family and knew if it weren't for him, I would have never had them. I was not getting paid a lot to be there, and since I was the sole provider for my family, I had to get back to work, and there was a massive project in the works all Because of Burt …

... WAKING UP IN RENO

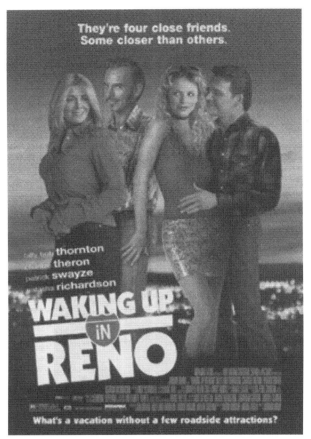

Because of Burt I met Billy Bob Thornton on *Evening Shade*, and he was a relatively unknown superstar in the making, but his immense talent foreshadowed his successful destiny.

There were few guest stars on the show I felt compelled to go on and on about how great they were. Not because they weren't great, but because Billy Bob Thornton was just over the top great. He was so humble and kind.

Later Linda Bloodworth Thomason hired my friend and writing partner Brent to do his homeless man from *The Right To Remain Silent* on *Hearts Afire*. It was there where Brent and Billy hit it off.

Billy and Brent really bonded, and Billy hired Brent to do a little movie called *Sling Blade*. Wink. It was because of that movie that Brent had the acting bug again. As that movie wrapped and was going to be edited and entering festivals Billy approached Brent and me at the Sportsman's Lodge in Sherman Oaks over drinks, about us writing a redneck version of *Bob Carol Ted and Alice*.

He said if we wrote it he thought he could sell it.

I was washing cars in Marion Indiana, and Brent was working in the liquor store in Moberly Missouri, so we figured we had nothing to lose. We wrote it with real struggles that people genuinely go through with a lot of emotion, volatility, and comedy. Brent and I wrote it in two months, and I handed the script to Billy and literally the next day he called me and said, "I think I can sell it." Moved that he or anyone for that matter would read a script that fast ... what if he actually could sell it?

With Brent Briscoe, & Billy Bob Thornton. Billy is da man!

All of a sudden, the little movie he wrote, directed and starred in called *Sling Blade* came out. He won an Academy Award, and sure enough, Billy Bob Thornton sold *Waking Up In Reno* to Miramax in 1997. Call it luck, timing, Billy Bob – I call it God to put all the pieces together at the right time. I also say if it were anybody else giving the script to Miramax other than Billy Bob Thornton at that time it would not have sold. The timing was perfect, but it was Billy Bob Thornton. "**EVERYONE MATTERS**" and even though Billy Bob was a virtual unknown we believed in him and thank God, he believed in us and shortly after that he became the hottest guy on the planet. I was so excited to tell Burt because this was all happening Because of Burt.

We did financially very well on the script, and it was the biggest check either of us ever received until that point. What a blessing for my family and me. All of the struggles and now with one fell swoop we catch up for other years of struggling. Every major agency wanted to sign us, and we went with ICM that had the perfect combination of three incredible agents for us; Barbara Dreyfus, Nicholas Reed, and Leora Bloch. We also gained an astonishing entertainment attorney Todd Stern who looked out for us legally.

The first reading was at the Sportsman's Lodge, the same place Billy pitched us the idea. He and his buddy Dwight Yoakam were co-producers and both there. Billy asked Mary Steenburgen, Powers Booth, Barbara Hershey, and Bo Hopkins to read the leads. They were terrific! I was so grateful to them. Jon Gordan from Miramax was there, and so was Laura Dern who I worked with on *Citizen Ruth* was dating Billy Bob. She was so enthusiastic and supportive, and we were on to something special.

With Billy Bob Thornton being who he was and Harvey Weinstein and the Miramax machine behind this project seemingly every star in Hollywood wanted to do this movie.
Because of that Brent and I were a part of the massive "Hollywood **WAVE**" that is an indescribable force of such magnitude that can literally change an artist's life overnight. One can go from dud to stud in a heartbeat if the wave comes. Thanks to Billy (all Because of Burt) the wave was upon Brent and me.

Billy and Laura were talking about doing the movie with their friends Dennis Quaid and Meg Ryan. Of course, that would have been a blast. Billy was being offered everything under the sun and had lots to choose from. I learned that Hollywood was quick to buy something but slow to make it.

Miramax then had the talented Peter Berg attached to see if he wanted to direct it. Peter was smart, he was an actor who knew what he was doing behind the camera. *Very Bad Things* was so brilliantly shot and edited, and of course, the performances were great, but the film was way too dark for my liking. That was the purpose of the movie, however … to show how very bad things lead to very bad actions, but I was too young, stupid and opinionated to see that clearly. Peter called some of his friends for a table read for us all to hear.

Oh, just little names like Madonna, Cameron Diaz, and Woody Harrelson. WOW!!! WOW!!! We were blown away. They were great! Madonna went against type and was A-1. Cameron really helped us a lot as writers make her character better. She not only read the crap out of that part but did what great actors do … become the role and share what they see the character could expand on. She was dead on. Woody was Woody – Great!

Peter Berg was hot too and getting offers all over the place, so the movie that sold like that, and that every actor wanted to do was still on hold.

Then all of a sudden in the front page of Variety, The Hollywood Reporter and all over TV it was announced that Brad Pitt and Jennifer Anniston were attached to do *Waking Up In Reno* with director James Gray.

Pitt, Aniston may be 'Waking Up in Reno'

By CHRIS PETRIKIN and MICHAEL FLEMING

Pitt

Aniston

Offscreen mates Brad Pitt and Jennifer Aniston are in talks to pair onscreen for Miramax in the road-trip comedy "Waking Up in Reno."

James Gray, who helmed "Little Odessa" and Miramax's upcoming "The Yards," is also in talks to direct the pic written by Brent Briscoe and Mark Fauser.

While no deals are in place, sources said that reps for Pitt, Aniston and Gray are in serious talks with Miramax to fit the project into their respective schedules. Miramax declined comment.

Ben Myron, Billy Bob Thornton and Dwight Yoakam will produce along with Paul Feldsher. Co-scribe Briscoe is also an actor who most recently co-starred with Thornton in "A Simple Plan."

"Waking Up in Reno" follows the on-the-road exploits of two white trash couples venturing westward from Arkansas to a monster truck rally.

Pitt and Aniston have been looking for a project to do together for a few months. Both stars are understood to have free slots in their present schedules, but it's unclear whether "Waking Up" could come together before Aniston has to return to her NBC series "Friends."

Pitt, who last starred in "Meet Joe Black," is repped by CAA and Brillstein-Grey Entertainment; Aniston, last seen in Fox's "Office Space," is repped by CAA and 3 Arts Entertainment. Gray is repped by UTA.

These articles in Variety and the Hollywood Reporter caused tremendous hype for us. Brad Pitt, my college friend, and the girl I spotted on the MTM lot which I told my wife was going to be a big star ... Jennifer Anniston wanted to do our script. Those two literally brought in huge offers to Brent and me for other projects.

Another huge wave!!!! Courtesy of Brad Pitt. I owe him several beers from Harpo's at Mizzou for making this public. It helped my family more than he will ever know and I am grateful.

Reno had good dialogue and characters created. It would make for an excellent small movie, but we had better scripts – but that didn't matter.

Miramax flew Brent and me to New York to meet with James Gray and go over the script. James asked us to do a little homework assignment. He wanted us to break down all of the significant characters and basically rank their looks, their smarts, their abilities, their pros, and cons. Brent and I felt like, we are busy now writing and rewriting other movies we don't have time for this "busy work." We're not getting paid for it, and it seemed counterproductive since we already had a script that all of these actors wanted to do. What we discovered is that we were wrong again. If we didn't do what the director wanted it would not have been good, and he could have asked other writers to do a rewrite which is precisely what Brent and I were being paid to do on other scripts. We were also wrong because by doing this little exercise we were able to identify each character better and had subtle brush strokes to enhance each character. All the things that Cameron Diaz pointed out to us plus this outline strengthened a script that was already revered and sold.

James was a perfectionist and was working on doing reshoots on his own movie and didn't know when he could get to this one. Finding the timing to get the right director, with the right actors for the right script is always extremely hard to do. James could not break away, and this whole deal with Brad and Jennifer went away. Now we were back to the drawing board.

It was frustrating because my agent Laura Bloch told me that if we get this movie produced you will get a whole new "Hollywood wave" and we were already riding a big one, so the future looked bright.

I met with Billy and talked to him about directing *Sling Blade*, and in many ways, his advice contradicted Jimmy Stewart's advice. I asked Billy how he learned about the use of cameras, and he said … "I get great actors and set the camera up and let them act" and he did, and it worked. He told me sometimes the DP would want to put a branch of leaves in front of the camera to make the shot more interesting and Billy would say … "Nah, take that sh*t out of there." When you watch *Sling Blade* you can see that Billy crafted a great unique story with brilliant actors who just killed it and the simplicity of the camera made it that much more special. In the case of Peter Berg's *Very Bad Things,* the way it was shot and cut enhanced the look and feel to that movie. Both worked, but both were extremely different.

Along came Jordan Brady, a funny guy, who knew comedy. I saw a short he did that was well done, and Miramax was sold that they had their man. I was thrilled. Billy Bob Thornton's schedule cleared up, and he was now available to do the movie. The next one they cast was Charlize Theron, who was not as well-known back then to the world but was a part of a hot Hollywood wave. We were beyond lucky to have her in our movie. Billy had just finished directing *All The Pretty Horses* for Miramax and asked his star, Penelope Cruz, to play a small role, and she agreed. I'm not sure why Dwight Yoakam didn't do the movie, because I thought that was the original plan, but apparently, Patrick Swayze really wanted to do it, but Miramax wasn't sure. I was like Wow. Please do it! But it seemed like the same thing – Patrick Swayze, "Peoples Sexist man," with several huge movies, lost the "Hollywood wave" … Again, I am a fan of history and if someone can do something great once they are capable of doing it again if they have the right vehicle. I am one who refuses to get caught up in the wave because everyone matters. Sure, I rode it … but I never thought I was better than I was and felt I had better things to share before the wave, during the wave, and after the wave. The wave does not define you or does it? Eventually, Patrick kept lobbying for it and landed it.

Then we signed Natasha Richardson, an award-winning British actress who was going, redneck. Wow! It was game on. Miramax nabbed the legendary director of photography William Fraker to make the imagery look pretty.

Brent and I wrote the movie with Billy in mind as the character of Roy, but he wanted to play the other role of Lonnie Earl and went against type, and Patrick Swayze went against type too. Their choice to switch just goes to show you how diversified and talented they both are. We were set. A movie that sold three years earlier was about to take place.

With Ben Myron Producer, Brent and Billy Bob on the set of *Waking Up In Reno*

Brent and I wrote roles for us in the movie. Brent wanted to play the sheriff, and I wanted to play the bellhop. Jordan was beyond cool and agreed to cast us both, but he had someone for the bellhop. The hysterical David Koechner. Jordan said to me, you can still be in it – just write yourself into the sheriff's scene. So, I wrote a foil for Brent's character and a Sheriff that would get manipulated by the flirtatious role that Charlize Theron played.

On January 30th, 2000, we were in Reno Nevada. I remember the date because it was when my then St. Louis Rams were in the Superbowl. Miramax treated Brent and me great! I had a luxury suite that overlooked the city with a hot tub. Billy Bob invited us to a place to watch the game. This was a dream come true. Brent and I showed up to meet the impressive cast, and it was at a strip club. I was so honored to meet everyone, but selfishly I wanted to go back to my room to watch and hear the game and not get distracted by the beautiful Charlize Theron on one side and the lovely Natasha Richardson on the other and strippers everywhere. It wasn't their fault it was just too hard for me to concentrate. LOL. I joke about it, but I loved the Rams and had to hear it and see it. Brent and I went to my suite and drank a ton of beer and watched one of the most exciting games of all time.

The first day on the set Patrick would not come out of his trailer. Something was terribly wrong. Apparently, he was drinking and was at the point he couldn't function. The producers called his wife to fly out. On a movie set, time is money, and overtime is huge money!

Every second you waste can hurt your bottom line, and as hard as it is to get work, I just couldn't understand why an actor would do that to themselves. Needless to say, Patrick's wife came out and whatever magic she applied Patrick was First Class the rest of the way. A plus. Great guy!

With Patrick Swayze and Brent on the set.

The first day of shooting we received a check for the same amount we sold the movie for. Oh my gosh! Brent and I gave each other the biggest hug. Two friends from Mizzou, who acted together, went down to Burt's, decided to write together, and now we're on a major Hollywood picture celebrating our dream come true.

Natasha Richardson's character was the rooting interest to see if she could wake up in Reno and realize what she had and take control of her destiny. Billy Bob played the slick car dealer who was charismatic to the public but lonely inside. Charlize Theron played the volatile best friend who was having a nuclear meltdown of guilt and Patrick played the naïve best friend who just was along for the ride. They were all terrific. I mean great! Not only great actors but great people that I enjoyed being with.

Our stellar cast! Billy Bob Thornton, Natasha Richardson, Charlize Theron, Patrick Swayze.

As a writer/actor, everyone treated me fantastic. However, something I learned, unlike plays where no actor, director or anyone changes a word of the script, and, unlike the television writers who usually have final say on everything, the movie scripts are different. Even though I was now an above the line person ... which meant credit wise and paycheck wise I had power, I really didn't have any say. Once the script sells to a studio, it is their property. They can shoot it as is, have it rewritten, use it for toilet paper or do whatever they want with it.

There is an art to writing something good enough and subtle enough that inspires people to visualize their own concept and yet be specific enough that they can't botch things that may be obvious to the writer but not others.

Brent and I drank a lot of beer in college and so the tradition continues on film.

After our scene, Brent and I left to go work on our other projects, so we did not see the rest of the movie being shot, but I was curious what the norm would be.

Meaning, we were the architects of the entire piece. If it were me, I would want to sit down with the writers and go over it scene by scene to see what their thoughts and visions were. Discover what was not spelled out as well, or what didn't work so we could work with them to enhance it. What was the goal of every scene to see if we needed it or we could tell it in a more efficient economical way? What was their song choices and why? It is so hard to get the right actors, the right crew, the right director the right script the right everything and put the puzzle together and once it starts it goes at warp speed. It's a miracle these things even get done.

When we were sent the first cut, I was devastated. I loved the acting, but there were gaping holes in the story, scenes that weren't even shot and it looked like we were just going for laughs. The exact opposite problem we had in *The Right To Remain Silent*. As an architect, if you take out a scene or a structural beam, you create an unstable house of cards that could fall.

With Charlize and Patrick from our scene in *Waking Up In Reno*.

Some scenes turned out funnier than what we wrote, and that is kudos to the director and actors, etc.... there were some hilarious moments and some powerful scenes that matched, in my mind, perfectly and again credit to the great acting and directing. That is so magical when writers sit by themselves in a room and write something you visualize, and it comes to life with all of the working parts around it.

Charlize Theron was truly brilliant and based on the rough scenes I saw; Jon Gordon and I were talking about her being nominated she was that good. Sadly, a lot of her stuff was cut and, in some cases, not even shot. Charlize is a major talent, and I am not only very impressed with her as an actress, but she's a very cool gal too.

The movie sadly didn't come close to the mark, and I knew it was in trouble before it was released. The first cut was rough (which is normal) and Brent and I were deeply concerned. They fired the editor and hired another one. The second cut was a lot closer to the vision, and we felt we had a real chance for success, but then for whatever reason, we regressed in the final cut in my humble opinion. Who knows who makes the calls, I was just happy to be along for the ride, and you learn that in movies the writer is usually done once it is sold.

It's incredible how many A-list actors wanted to do our script and when it came out how much criticism we as writers received on the script from critics who I feel quite certain NEVER read the script. I was blessed to be on a beautiful wave of excitement for a while and so honored that this cast and studio did the movie. It paid for my home, but as an artist, it hurt. The bottom line is that there are a lot of things that go into making a movie and who knows why it derailed. That is the magic and mystery of movie making.

The Weinstein's invited Julie and me to one of their Academy Award parties, and that was the last time I saw Patrick Swayze. We saw each other on the red carpet, and he gave me a huge hug. The Paparazzi started snapping pictures like crazy and asked who I was. When they were told I was the writer, the cameras went down indifferently. A friend of mine later said, "At least you are on this side of the ropes on the red carpet." That night at the party I spent the majority of my time in-between Walter Cronkite, and Limp Bizkit at the bar and we had the greatest conversation. Think of that threesome. Surreal!

Julie and I ready to go to an Academy Award party.

What an experience this movie was. I am saddened by Patrick Swayze and Natasha Richardson's untimely deaths. Both class acts – but I feel like the luckiest guy in the world to have a vision come to life – because of that vision, to be able to employ so many people and make people laugh to this day. Getting residual checks is nice too. This miracle adventure was spawned by Billy Bob Thornton. We had the chance to meet him and work with him Because of Burt …

... BILLY BOB THORNTON

Billy Bob Thornton is the real deal! A genuine all-around great artist. His delivery and wit are fantastic, and the fact that he was just a regular guy who loved the St. Louis Cardinals made him even that much more appealing to me. He was encouraging and thoughtful. Billy broke any stereotype or typecasting which allowed him to play the many diversified roles we enjoy watching him play.

That is not easy, but he does it with seemingly great ease and no "Hollywood façade." He just is Billy ... which to me makes him so interesting and appealing. Billy is great with comedy which is the hardest thing to do ... but has a massive range. Other than Burt Reynolds Billy Bob was the biggest game-changer for us. His belief in us lead to so many jobs. He not only started the WAVE ... he put us on his magic surfboard and changed our lives.

He helped Brent find part of his instrument again. Brent all but gave up acting, and if you saw what I saw at Mizzou and in other shows, it was a crime that he would give it up. Brent was so talented he just needed someone to pick him up. Billy hired him a multitude of times and gave Brent the love for acting again.

I'm going to fast forward several years or so. I later became the Executive Director of a not-for-profit called the Community School of the Arts and wanted to see if Billy would make a short public service announcement for my school for free. My friend was also directing a movie and asked me to contact Billy to see if he would act in the film for one day and make $250 thousand for a day's worth of work. I asked Billy on both, and he turned down the $250,000 but was willing to do the commercial for me for free. Simply amazing. Simply Billy Bob Thornton. I have let him know many times how grateful I am to him and what an impact he has made on my family for believing in us and giving us this incredible opportunity. Thank you, Billy Bob Thornton ... who I met ... Because of Burt ...

... MADISON

Because of Burt, I met my wife and one of her best friends Cathy Bindley. Her husband Bill Bindley cast me in one of my first movies *Freeze Frame*, with Shannen Doherty. Bill gave me the *Madison* script (which was then called *Rooster Tail*) that he and his brother Scott wrote. I read it on the plane and loved it. It's a great family movie based on a true story, and I really took to the character of Travis. I told Bill how passionate I was to play him and ten years later I received a call from my friend Bill who told me I had the role.

I was thrilled! His casting director didn't think I was physically right for the role, based on my look ... She was right.

But Bill knew me, and I so appreciated his loyalty, kindness, and faith that I could pull it off. I was instrumental in getting my writing partner Brent Briscoe cast too.

I did heed the concern of the casting director and decided I would not come out of my trailer without my glasses, hat, and accent.

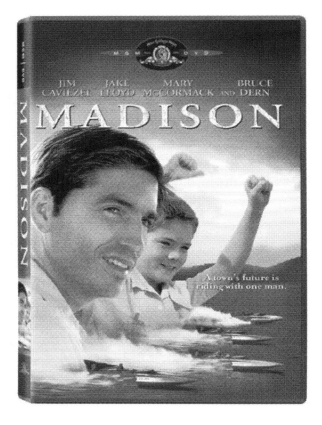

It was imperative that I convinced the cast and crew that I was Travis and not some guy who was just "acting."

Travis was a sweet character, but a little off and being the good person that Jim Caviezel was, he didn't run away from me, but instead, he sat next to me during lunch and introduced himself. We acted and sat next to each other for an entire week.

On Friday night we had our first cast party, and I felt that I could now be me. I could now drop the glasses, accent, and hat and just have a good time. Jim Caviezel came over to me and introduced himself, and I told him "I have been acting with you all week long." He was confused. Was I an extra? "Jim, I am Travis." and he couldn't believe it. To see his face was one of the highest compliments I have ever received. From that point on I was in with the cast and the crew.

Thanks to Director and friend Bill Bindley for believing in me for the role of Travis. His casting Director did not think I was right based on my headshot and look, but she didn't know how nerdy I was.

Madison was a real family affair, and we had a blast. The town was terrific and beautiful. Seeing some of the people we would portray were inspiring and we felt an obligation to do them and the town justice and honor this great story.

By being friends with Burt Reynolds gave me a considerable advantage and street credit on the set with other actors. Mary McCormick had just finished doing a movie with Burt so there was that connection. Paul Dooley was on *Evening Shade*, so we had that connection.

Burt's great friendship with Bruce Dern made such a seamless transition to all of us. Acting with Bruce Dern was fun as well. Even though we knew of each other through his daughter Laura Dern and the whole Billy Bob Thornton connection he was still intimidating as an actor. Our first meeting in the movie was completely improvised. Bruce's character came over to my character/me and told me to clean all of the parts … I went with it and said "Okay,"

"No! Not okay … just do it!"…

And I (really was nervous) and said "Okay" and got a big laugh from the crew and we couldn't use that take. But Bill and his brother Scott (the other co-writer) were so gracious they said keep it and do it again and it's in the film.

Jim Caviezel, Jake Lloyd, me and Frank Knapp in Madison.

While making this movie, Brent and I were doing a rewrite for Universal Studios, and Bob Simonds called *Fool Proof*. It was an exhilarating time knowing we were acting in a movie, rewriting another studio picture and were a few months away from shooting *Waking Up In Reno*. We would write in our trailers, write in our hotel rooms, study our lines, act when it was go time and go out and have a great time balancing everything.

The crew was hard working and had challenges with old vintage boats. There would be times where the boats were working and were so loud that the 2nd unit had to capitalize and everything else had to stop. Then if one boat had some technical issues, the actors would race to the location and shoot the scene while we had the opportunity. Bill, our director, was battling boat issues and less light in the day because we shot in September.

He had young Jake Lloyd who had to be in school x-amount of the day. It was not easy so any chance I could help Bill or our AD's, push our team along I would. Bill pulled it off in a big way, and the cast was fantastic, and we were all very close.

With Brent, Frank, and Bruce Dern in-between takes.

One of the things that Burt taught Brent and I was to be kind to everyone. "Everyone matters," so we were in a financial position to treat the entire cast and crew to bowling, food, and drinks to set a tone early that we were all family.

... JIM CAVIEZEL

I love Jim Caviezel, and we hung out a lot. I can't stress enough what a good person he is. The lead actor and director set a tone of a movie, and I was allowed to be myself as the clown on the set to keep everybody light, happy and working hard.

To this day we still talk about the fun we had. Jim and I have stayed in touch, and when the timing is right, he told me he wants to star in my movie *Bite Me* about a Vampire who wants to go to Heaven. Again, Hollywood often gets a bad knock and the people within it, but Jim is one of the really good guys. When Brent died Jim called me right away and wanted me to come out and stay with his family. He has a beautiful family that I adore, and we had a blast together even though it was under tough circumstances losing Brent. Then when Burt died, I received a call right away from Jim, and that is a true friend. I love good people, and Jim Caviezel is a good person with a great heart.

... BACK TO MADISON

Chelcie Ross was in *Hoosiers* and now *Madison* that made it a treat for people in Indiana. He did

With Brent and Chelcie Ross

Waking Up In Reno with us. Chelcie came to Marion to see the Premiere of *Madison* and stayed with me. There was a huge party for him and the movie at our friends the Gorman's house.

Paul Dooley 2nd to the right.

I had an all-night chat session with Mary McCormack who was as hip as you could get. Mary's a legit, committed actress who was money.

The Crew standing next to our boat Miss Madison.

We spent a lot of time at Shipley's bar relaxing and at the end of the day.

My wife and I went to the Premiere in Madison, and it was a joy to see the cast, the crew, and community again.

Many years later I was asked to be The Grand Marshall of the annual Madison Indiana Regatta parade. I brought my family to be a part of that majestic community. A Rooster Tail is a big **WAVE** that a racing boat causes, but I would be on a series of powerful waves … which would have only been possible Because of Burt …

... HILLBILLY HEIST

A successful producer named Kevin Messick approached Brent and me about writing a movie based on a true story about the second largest bank heist in US history, performed by the funniest, wackiest bunch ever. We read the story and fell in love with it.

We went to Miramax, where his former wife (Jill Messick) was our friend and a terrific person/producer and Executive at Miramax. Brent and I were hot at the time and were extremely confident. We pitched our vision for Act I then Act II and told them Act III writes itself. We finished our pitch and thanked them and left.

My agent Barbara Dreyfus told me she wanted double for what we received in *Waking Up In Reno*, I said, "Whoa, I would be happy with what we had." She said, in her typical Barbara way, "Shut up and trust me."

"But -"

"Just buy me a pair of shoes when it's all done." And she hung up. I looked at my wife stunned, confused, concerned, uncertain ... then I received a call from the producer Kevin Messick, who told me it's not going to work because we asked for too much.

Dammit, I was in a complete whirlwind, and before I could say anything, Barbara called in, and I clicked over to her, and she said, "Okay, it's done. I told you. Just buy me a pair of shoes."

"WHAT??!! Kevin is on the other line and said it wasn't going to work because you asked for too much."

"Tell him to F*ck off and buy me a pair of shoes. It's done. You got what I asked for." She hung up on me again, and I clicked back over to Kevin to tell him what she said ... I left out the f-bomb. Kevin was thrilled, and it was on.

With Producer Kevin Messick and Brent in front of the Loomis Fargo truck in North Carolina that helped move 17 million dollars.

Miramax flew us down to North Carolina to meet the FBI, some of the bank robbers, and to see where they went from a trailer to a mansion. It was a great story. When we pitched the idea, we saw it through the eyes of the mastermind. The pressure that was on him to not get caught and keep the 21 other people he had under his wing to not squeal or do something stupid was fascinating. When we interviewed the FBI, we were so impressed and intrigued with them. We met with them for two days and went over everything. It was remarkable the challenges and stories they had. It was so rich with the material we did it from two perspectives on opposite ends that were on a collision course towards each other. It was a long first draft but was very funny and real! Kevin gave us notes, and we went at it for another re-write which was part of the contract.

When it finished our other agent Leora Bloch, said this was her favorite script and that it would be huge. Billy Bob Thornton liked it as well, but his girlfriend really loved it and wanted to direct it, and fortunately, I had already met her Because of Burt ...

... LAURA DERN

Laura is indeed one of the sweetest people you would ever meet. She comes from a phenomenal pedigree of actors and yet she has successfully carved out her own mark as an iconic award-winning actress. She is humble beyond words, grounded and a student of the industry. Laura was looking for new challenges like directing. I met her on the set of *Citizen Ruth*, and then again in the table read of *Waking Up In Reno*. She was on the set of Reno a lot, and I had just finished working with her dad on Madison. Laura's mom Diane Ladd, optioned Rich Petrofsky's and my movie *Chasing Roger Maris* three times for her to play the lead role in. Bottom line, there was a whole family connection for us with Laura and her family. Laura really loved the *Hillbilly Heist* script and had her eyes set on directing it. How thrilling to have an award-winning actress with the experience of Laura at the helm and with her partner Billy Bob (our buddy) building a stellar cast.

Brent and I met Laura for lunch on a Thursday at the Beverly Hills Hotel talking about the script and trying to figure out how we were going to take it to the next level.

We talked about assembling a table read as we did with Reno and show them that she could bring the talent. The script was ready to go, and we had an inspiring meeting. On that Sunday, I was watching the news and heard that Billy Bob was with Angelina Jolie. Wow! There went that. The next year, I received a Christmas card from Billy Bob and Angelina. Then Brad Pitt wound up with Angelina??? Small world. Anyway, the following year I was at Sundance with some of the cast from the movie *Madison*. Bruce Dern, Laura's dad, was downright mean to me about Billy Bob. Of course, Burt taught me how to stand up for myself, and I knew I didn't do anything wrong. Bruce wrote me a nice apology letter later, and all was forgiven. It does me no good to get involved and pick sides and get into the weeds with their personal situation. It's none of my business, and the best thing I could do was love and respect both of them.

The movie had lots of different writers and twists and turns. It was eventually made with a great cast in a movie called *Masterminds*. The Writers Guild of America usually gives the original writers the credit which means money forever. However, since this was a true story, apparently there could be a multitude of different takes on it, and therefore there was no obligation to honor our original deal even though Kevin Messick was the producer for ours and *Masterminds*. We did get paid handsomely to write it but getting another huge pop and residuals forever would have been so much better. Respectfully speaking, the true story was so much funnier than the movie. For some reason, they took so many liberties and had so many untruths that it was hard for me to watch. The real story was great, and it's such a shame they didn't honor it because they had a great cast.

Brent and I were going to be able to rewrite others too and were riding a successful **WAVE** that at times almost capsized us, but never lost sight that we were in this game clearly Because of Burt …

... SUCCESSES AND ODDITIES

Brent and I were hired to do a rewrite of a movie for Dimension called *The Buddy System*, and again we have to thank Bob Weinstein for this wonderful opportunity. We were taught early on by our agents and Todd Stern, our entertainment attorney that we could make a great living being script doctors. We had *The Right To Remain Silent,* Evening *Shade* and *Waking Up In Reno*, but we're looking for more originals like *Hillbilly Heist.* As opportunities came our way like *The Buddy System,* we would take them and do our best to put them in a situation to go into production.

Being that we were currently labeled as the king of writing "rednecks," our agents hooked us up with an actor who was on a huge **WAVE** like we were ... Orlando Jones. Orlando is a fun guy, and at the time he was as hot as it gets. He was acting and selling many projects. Orlando had an idea called *Redneck*, it was a dark comedy about him playing an African American being raised by the Klan. Here was this black young man, who hated blacks, gays, Jews, everything and decided he wanted to go to college. The redneck racists parents reluctantly let him go. His character winds up rooming with a gay guy who becomes his best friend and falls in love with an African American woman who he thinks has the same "skin condition" he does ... until they awaken him to the fact that he was black. He then finds out he was adopted. His biological mom was Jewish, and his biological dad was black and the head of the NAACP. Everything he thought he hated he was. The Klan family genuinely loved him, but so did everyone else and it was a battle to see what side the redneck would pick to declare his love.

I liked it because of its inherent darkness and comedy, but more importantly the ability to make everyone think how ridiculous racism is, and to respect diversity. To me, it's not brushing racism under the carpet but exposing it for all of its stupidity. Orlando, Brent and I went to several studios to pitch it. I remember Mike Deluca heard our pitch and told us it was the most offensive thing he ever heard. I respectfully could see that if you don't know what our point was, but we wanted to take a **RISK**. It was dangerous, and we were willing to live on the edge knowing our hearts and our hope for the world to get it was in the right place. We went to Columbia Pictures and pitched the idea and boom. They loved it and bought it. BOOM BABY! There's another one sold.

Brent and I were so excited because we saw that we could be equal opportunity offenders and bring it home to have tremendous social relevance of the insanity of racism. We were writing it and moving forward. A big six-figure paycheck was coming our way, and things were great. We were doing a lot of writing/acting, and Orlando was in a significant role.

We talked to Orlando, and he started to get cold feet on his concept. The idea he had was definitely risky - no question and that was before the country became even so politically correct. We saw Mr. Deluca's response. What if it would backfire? Regardless, Orlando was trying to take the edge off and change what we sold. We had a signed deal with Columbia, but we were in this for the long haul. I respect and like Orlando. We were grateful he believed in us to write it, and we think we would have killed it, but the way society is today that movie might have killed us. Maybe Orlando was right. Brent and I made an unbelievable unheard of moral decision to not take the money from Columbia. I genuinely feel they respected us a lot for doing the right thing.

Robert Simonds is such a cool producer, and I always liked meeting with him. He gets up and starts pacing the room and pitches. We came close to doing each other's work before, but now we were hired by him and Universal Studios to do a rewrite of a movie called *Foolproof.* Great paycheck and a lot of it came from the Brad Pitt and Jennifer Anniston hype of doing Reno. Mr. Simonds wanted to beat the rush of *Ocean's Eleven* which was in the works, but this was the crazy comedic version of it. He had Martin Lawrence to play the lead, and that was exciting for us. We were big fans of Martin. Brent and I were acting on *Madison* during our writing of that film and had fun writing it. We created some excellent characters to go along with what was in the script and felt we had Martin Lawrence's voice. We submitted the script, and Bob had some notes for us. We were ready to address them, and then Martin Lawrence went into a coma from heat exhaustion. The project died. WOW! You can't write this stuff.

Paramount Studios hired us to rewrite the infamous Joe Eszterhas's movie *Male Pattern Baldness* which he received 2 million dollars against 4.5 for the script. Rewriting this high-priced script by this Hollywood legend, was a true honor. It gave us a lot of street credit, and we nailed it. The producers Donald De Line and Wendy Japhet really liked the script, the studio wanted it too, and I think they knew Joe Eszterhas's book was coming out. If his book was successful, they were going to ride the wave. The book wasn't successful, but Joe was/is an elite, successful screenwriter, and nobody could ever take that away from him. We really liked the script and wanted Billy Bob Thornton to do it. We wanted Burt to play his dad. The **WAVE** that Billy was on died down a bit, and that's how fickle the town was/is, and they were into James Gandolfini. Either way, it was out of our hands, but we enjoyed rewriting it, enjoyed the money, and it helped us get another job later.

Columbia was kind enough to want to hire us again, I think from our ethics prior too on *Redneck* and how we scripted *Male Pattern Baldness.* This rewrite was for a movie called *Pearls Before Swine.* We were working with Carrie Richmond, who was terrific.

At the same time, we were hired by Universal Studios and Tom Shadyac and Michael Bostick, two great high character guys that I really enjoyed working with. They invited us to the premiere of *Bruce Almighty.* We were paid handsomely to rewrite *Crossdressing* three times. It's not what it sounds like, but a funny, smart movie that again has a cool moral message.

We were writing two movies at once, getting paid a lot of money and blessed beyond belief. Things were great on that front. Brent was acting more which was excellent but drinking a lot more and was newly married to a porn star that was truly troubled. The business was working really good for Brent when it came to acting and writing, but his relationship with this **MONSTER** was toxic to him, me, and everyone around. Brent would show up drunk to some of our studio meetings and proudly tell them he was married to a porn star, but then Brent called me up to seek my advice.

Brent told me his wife asked him to go to a porn awards show in Vegas and said "what if she wins … what do I say? Congrats you sucked the best d*ick?" You can't write this stuff. Our agent was calling me telling me I had to do something about him. Me? I'm his friend and partner. I love him, but I'm trying to help him, as I have done before. Here's the funny thing … it was role reversal now … he was doing movies now and making more money than me so therefore in everybody's mind, he was right, and I was wrong. Yet this was getting worse and how can you tell someone who is doing better than you in the business he was hurting us? I was Sonny, and he was Cher. I didn't want to be Sonny, but I couldn't convey to Cher "I Got You, Babe," but we're in a lot of trouble if we don't change our ways. He was buying her horses and more horses, and they were not cheap.

We would be on the phone discussing work, and she would get on and say "From now on I'm your partner. You need to go through me." I would get off the phone quickly with that drunken dumb ass.

My mom had unexpectedly passed away November 23 of 2001, and it was devastating. She was supposed to get out of the hospital on November 22nd, and we were going to have Thanksgiving together. That morning things turned for the worse, and I sadly watched her die. I took 3 days off to organize my mom's funeral and then was back to work. No flowers, no how are you? You okay? It was sad and cold.

We turned in both scripts. *Pearls Before Swine,* it died too, but *Crossdressing* was very much alive. They loved our rewrite and wanted another. Brent called me up and told me he didn't want to write anymore. Here we are living the great American dream, and my mom just died, and now he wants to quit writing in the middle of a huge six-figure deal? Was this because of the pressure? The alcohol or the porn wife who all of a sudden went from getting screwed for a living to try to screw Brent and me? Barbara Dreyfus would always call me and tell me I had to do something, and I was becoming bitter. Why didn't she talk to him? I didn't want to do more work trying to figure out how to navigate between that disease and the monster he was with.

Every March, my wife, and family would go to Jupiter Florida where we met and where Julie's dad had a place. It was the perfect time for me to escape the insanity that sadly overcame our partnership. Usually, every March I would get together with Burt Reynolds too and either I would go to one of his acting classes, we would go out to eat and catch up or hang at his house. This time, I knew that Burt loved both Brent and I. It just would not be fair for me to vomit on Burt about what was going on, so it was the one time I didn't contact him. Later in the week, I received a call from Burt for me to come over. I was so happy to hear from him and wondered how he knew I was there. Any time I could see or hear from Burt; it was just what the doctor ordered. Burt invited me out to eat, and we went to dinner to catch up. He was just so proud of our accomplishments but then brought up his concern for Brent. Burt told me that Brent and his wife came to his gate at the house and sounded so drunk Burt wouldn't answer. He wondered what was wrong. Burt was very loving to me and protective. He had seen this so many times in his career and was sensitive to Brent too. It was like a coach, teacher, and friend that encouraged me to keep pushing on and was concerned that Brent was getting gobbled up by the **" MONSTER."**

I was a few months removed from my mom dying. I lost my partner in Brent, and the ever-caring Burt Reynolds called me up and took me out to eat to comfort me. I love that man and miss him.

Brent and I were no longer talking, and we had a planned meeting to go meet with producer Michael Bostick. I felt obligated to fly to Los Angeles and take the meeting and tell Michael that either I would finish the rewrite, or he did not have to pay us if that was his choice. I needed to come clean either way.

Brent wound up showing up too and looked worse for wear. Two people, in the waiting room that have been partners in college, roommates, great friends, traveled to different cities together, worked together, knew each other's thoughts and were not even talking to each other. His dark road was his business, and I would always be there for him, but I had a family and a responsibility to take care of them. We didn't say a word to each other and when we were called into Michael's office … we did some of the best acting we've ever done. We had it all figured out how we were going to better the script, and we finished each other's sentences, and it was classic Mark and Brent. We left that meeting and received another rewrite, but I laid down the law if we were going to continue and he agreed.

It was shortly after that that the monster left him, and he lost a small fortune. I felt so sorry for him and loved him. It was no doubt the best thing for him, and we had other projects going. I had my third child … Jack Fauser … what a blessing.

I did a pilot for my friend Tommy Thompson. He liked the Elvis character I played in the play at Burt's dinner theater and gave me a twist as a psychotic bank robber. It was a pilot called *Fire Beach*.

Elvis Bank robber – originally seen at Burt's Theater and now is in a pilot *Fire Beach*.

I was writing on my own and with Rich Petrofsky. I was open to writing with Brent again if he was willing to do the work.

My agent made it clear that they didn't want Brent as a writer or me as a writer - they wanted Mark and Brent. So, the movie that Rich and I did, *A Matter of Time*, was pitched to our agent saying it was written by Brent and I and this guy named Rich. Well, as long as Brent and I were on it, she was game, and she loved the pitch. She set up meetings with several hot producers who had a different studio deal with various studios and every single producer flipped. Barbara told us this was huge, and we were going to make a fortune. To me, it was so fake, because Brent didn't write a word, but we were using the perception to appease "the wave." Rich was willing to go for it because one-third of something is a lot better than a half of nothing. Barbara set meetings up every day with different producers and different studios. Never had we had something with this much hype from so many different people? Brent and I went into our first meeting and did exactly what we did with everybody else who loved it. We didn't even get to the car, and we received a call from our agent, Barbara Dreyfus, saying it's done. "You mean, they want it, and you got a deal?"

"Nope. They didn't want it, and you're not going to sell it." We were stunned. We have a batting average of 1,000, and now we have one person saying no, and that means she's giving up? Barbara said, "I'm just saying it's not going to sell?" Now to this day, I never knew what that meant? Why is one "no" going to dictate all of the yesses we received the week before? It's all about the **WAVE**, and Barbara predicted a puddle now, and it left me so confused and angry. "If you don't believe in it anymore just cancel the rest of the meetings," I said.

"Nah, just go do them anyway." It was like I know you are going to be told no but just for the fun of it do it anyway and get rejected. It made no sense. The only thing I could ever come up with is that if the first person said "Yes" that would give her leverage to start the **WAVE** and make us all big money. But to me, all it took was one person to believe in us to get a break and sell it. Like the way Burt Reynolds did for us or Billy Bob Thornton or my sister-in-law or Tommy Thompson or the other studios that hired us. All it takes is one. Brent and I made the sacrifice against all the odds because we wanted to be artists for a living. That is what we were. If you believe in the ART … and she did, then fight for what you believe in. Needless to say, Babs was right. She knew the game, and the fix was in. Mind numbing.

The incredible producer Cathy Konrad came to us on a rewrite she wanted us to do for Columbia and asked our thoughts on a script. We read it and gave her our take, and she loved it. She took us in to see the same buyer who we sold *Redneck* and *Pearls Before Swine* too, and we all felt great. We gave the buyer our entire pitch from beginning to end in a detailed way, and we knew we sold it. In fact, he told us he wanted it right there in the room. It was all but done until … "Before I go down the hall to pitch it to our marketing people help me put it into a thirty-second commercial."

I was stupid, dumb, stubborn, flabbergasted. WHAT???! We gave him more than a commercial we gave him the entire movie. Why do we have to now give him a thirty-second commercial? Do we need to sweep the bathrooms too or blow little people because we can do that too?

There was now a new variable to deal with in the Hollywood Studio world, and that was "Marketing." The buyer could no longer buy the movie and give it to the marketing department to figure out how to market it. Now the marketing would dictate to the buyer if that concept could be marketed for success. It actually makes good business sense but was very foreign to us at the time. Those were the new rules, and the buyer started to reconstruct our entire script to fit the 30-second commercial he needed to sell. The movie worked, and he knew it but to make it fit in a 30-second box was a house of cards. When you took that out, then this goes away. If you do that – then this alters that. It was a hot mess. The industry changed before our eyes. Movies like *Sling Blade* would be harder to make under these new scenarios of marketing. Obscure movies would more than likely not be made by studios as much. If you have a Marvel character, they could market that. Star Wars yup! Michael Myers from Halloween yup! In retrospect, it made total sense, and the success of the industry proves the value of marketing. I learned a lot from that. A lot … but I would have far preferred the money and learned that lesson later.

... BRENT BRISCOE

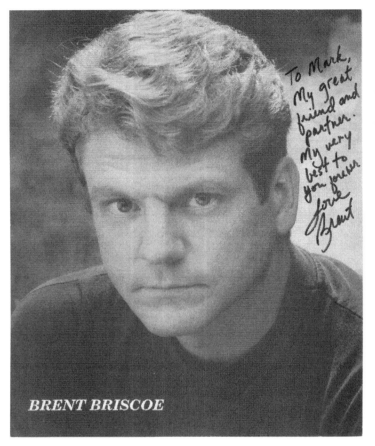

If one has chapters in their life, then Brent Briscoe is a book in my life. College roommates, acting partners - to the point we could finish each other's sentences. We were blessed to have great teachers and fellow classmates at Mizzou who molded us and made us better actors. Plays we did won awards in Kansas City and at the Kennedy Center in Washington DC. *Eleven Zulu* won more American College Theater Festival awards than any other play at the time. It was like winning the National Championship. A stellar College career that was memorable. So many laughs - So many stories.

One thing to note: our Teachers like Jim Miller, Weldon Durham, Larry Clark, and Richard Klepac extracted things from Brent that Hollywood never saw. Brent showcased his diversified mass talent that those of us there were so honored to see. He could sing, dance, transform into anything. He was a true actor! We were lucky to be a part of Burt Reynolds Institute for Theater Training with all of the former apprentices and teachers like Burt Reynolds, Charles Nelson Reilly, and Dom DeLuise. They were incredible to pay it forward and give us a work ethic second to none and bond amongst all apprentices that will never be broken.

Charles Nelson Reilly dared us to write, and so we did, and the great Burt Reynolds had us do our play *The Right To Remain Silent* that lead to so many other things. Burt then hired us over and over again. So many great stories there. We met Billy Bob Thornton because of Burt and Billy changed the game for us. We struck Gold. We landed big agents in Hollywood who were able to get us work left and right.

Brent on the left – our wonderful teacher/director from Mizzou Jim Miller and I.

The success was a dream come true, but the memories and laughter were even better.

For all of the people at Mizzou, Moberly, Burt Reynolds Institute, Jupiter Florida, Los Angeles, *Evening Shade, Madison*, *Waking Up In Reno* and the circle of friends of Brent celebrate Brent Briscoe. Those that genuinely knew him know he is now at peace. The thing I hold onto is now he knows how much he was loved.

For the million phone calls we had together I would always start it off by saying ...."Breeeeeeeeeeeeeeeeeeeeent" So for the last time "Breeeeeeeeeeeeeeeeeeeent" Your partner loves you... But now you know. Rest my friend peacefully and save me a spot ...

I needed a break from Hollywood and was in a position to give back Because of Burt ...

... COMMUNITY SCHOOL OF THE ARTS

Burt built a theater/school that brought me so much in my life. I also remembered the conversation I had with him in gratitude as to why he did so much for me. "Because Jimmy Stewart did it for me and someday, I want you to do it for others." Around 2002, I was financially in pretty good shape and needed to break away from LA for a bit. The cost of living in Marion Indiana and lifestyle of my 3 acres of land compared to my small one-bedroom apartment in Santa Monica was a night and day difference. Sure, I missed the weather, excitement, and friends in Los Angeles, but the art offerings were not something that inspired me at the time in Los Angeles. The people in Marion were great too, and my family lived there. If my wife was kind enough to come on the LA journey with me for eight years, I could make the best out of her hometown. Up until then, other than coaching my kid's little league team, I was not active in the community and didn't make a difference.

I was asked to participate as a board member for the Marion Community School of the Arts which was housed in a basement of a church and taught six classes or so a year.

The Community helped build one of the real gems in our county now known as CSA. Total team effort.

Marla Keppler was a friend and community gem who was running it and paid for the phone line to come to her house. There was tremendous talent in the community ... talent on par with what I saw in Los Angeles, but not harnessed. The community suffered from a significant self-esteem issue. It was once a big factory town, known for its high school basketball State Championships. With factories gone and having the highest poverty rate in the State, the city needed a new identity to recreate themselves or their small town would continue to die.

There were a lot of successful people here, good, hard-working people. Marion is where James Dean was born, and he was raised in Fairmount which is our county. Jim Davis, the creator of Garfield, was also born and raised in the county.

Cole Porter used to take a train from Peru to downtown Marion to take piano lessons. Marion and Grant County have a rich history in the arts, and I wanted to help add on to that.

Being from a big city, I didn't understand some of the small-town dynamics. I would watch a car dealer look inside someone's garage to see what they were driving, and it was personal. I would learn that where you went to go grocery shopping, where you eat, where you dance, where you went to school was all personal.

I loved the quaintness of the town and the people. If I could respectfully get them to see their potential. Do what Burt Reynolds did and build an art school and showcase the greatness of the county, the sky could be the limit for them. I saw little Silver Dollar City in Missouri before it became Branson Missouri. It's all in the mindset and direction the county collectively chooses to go in.

I was asked to serve on the board, and I could never be Burt, but he wanted us to pay it forward, and now it made sense. I made a decision to take a year off of Hollywood and try to serve as a board member and make a difference in my small way.

With a thousand dollars in the school's account and the church ready to close, my time of service would be short-lived if we couldn't find a place. The first thing I did was to go on a complete cold call to a real estate guy I saw all over the place named Maidenberg. Frank Maidenberg was kind enough to meet with me, and I told him my story and my objectives. Little did I know how philanthropic he was. He was one of those people that built many organizations and loved hard-working dreamers. Frank allowed us to go to one of his great creative facilities at The Centrum Mall. The rent was beyond reasonable, and we could survive if we had enough revenue from classes.

There were no employees at The Marion Community School of the Arts, so I did what Burt did in *The Longest Yard and* tried to find the best teachers we could find who would create their own curriculum. They would set their price, and we would house them, pay the utilities and get 30 percent. We had Stain glass class, painting, I was going to teach acting, and we would do pottery at the high school. I went to my kid's former dance teacher to see if she would want to teach. Let me stop to share a troubling scenario. As you can tell, I love and honor my teachers. I realize without them I never would have had the skill set, passion and drive to do what I do. One thing I found unsettling here was that a dance teacher who was trained from one studio left it and opened one to compete with the place that taught her. Then her people left her to open up another dance studio to compete with her. This pattern continued. I guess what goes around comes around, but she was so hurt she closed. I went to all of them to give my passionate plea that this small community needed to band together and if they do, we could make some noise and turn heads. If it's every person for themselves, we will all just be little fish in little ponds and stay a small dying town. United, we could make some serious waves.

I encouraged them to come on board, and I would do everything in my power to make them successful, promote them, market them, and build something special for kids and adults. It would be very healing to the small community to see everyone united. That is the power of art. One of them agreed, and the other chose not to. I was disappointed but understood and then focused on what we were going to do to help the community.

We had a small board of people that were a blessing; Marla was indeed known as the "founder" and loved the arts. She helped a lot of organizations like the Philharmonic and Meals on Wheels and anything else in the community she could assist. Her husband was a doctor, and it allowed her the financial means to be the great volunteer she was. Dawn Darga was the engine. A graphic designer and artist that would take the visions to paper. The lesson I learned from WWE great Vince McMahon and now Hollywood was the importance of marketing. We needed to brand ourselves .. instead of calling us the Marion Community School of the Arts ... We wanted to drop the Marion aspect because we wanted it to be for the entire county and beyond. Community School of the Arts or CSA would stick better. Dawn was and is a brilliant artist that would volunteer countless, and I mean countless hours to build this organization. Without her, it would have never been what it was. Beth Kachel was an accountant, willing to give countless hours to protect our limited resources and see over them as they grew.

We came up with a Go-Kart fundraiser that was like WWE meets car racing and the community rallied around us and we made $60,000 during one race.

Our Annual CSA Go-Art Go-Kart race was a race for the Arts!

We ascertained more dance teachers and more kids. I started shooting commercials using local businesses to participate so they could get a taste of the arts. Our local cable channel thanks to Inge Harte would air them nonstop all over the county. I asked my friend Ted McGinley who was doing *Hope and Faith* at the time if he would do a short PSA. He had Kelly Ripa, and Faith Ford join him, and it was huge. Billy Bob Thornton did one. Jim Caviezel did a commercial for the school, Haley Joel Osment, David DeLuise who was on *The Wizards of Waverly* did it, and people were going nuts. Those commercials started airing, and we were on fire. "Everyone matters" and I wanted my kids and community to know they mattered. The school was blowing up with success, and we had to hire people.

After working seventy plus hours a week for a year joyfully for free, my work was done. It was time for me to get back to work. My fellow board member and friend Darren Reese met me at, The Mill Restaurant, and said, "If you leave now, everything you worked so hard for will be for not." He then asked me if I would be the Executive Director of the school and they would pay 12 grand a year. I was not insulted I was almost moved to tears. CSA and Darren did not have twelve grand to pay me, and I knew it as a board member, but they believed in me to build it.

If you build it, they will come. I love money. I really do! But I have never been motivated by it … well, maybe a few times. ☺ But most of the things I work on are because I believe in the cause and am passionate about it. Therefore, I have always had **FAITH** that if you work hard, the money will come.

The reality was now in two years I would make twelve grand, and that is way beyond the poverty level. My wife stood by me and believed in the mission. She volunteered countless hours as well and did everything in her powers to make it successful. It was her hometown and our great team, and we were starting to make a profound difference.

We were making a lot of noise and big waves for our kids and community … thanks to Burt Reynolds.

One of the things I wanted the kids to do was CREATE their own stuff. Whether they wanted to be an actor/writer/singer/songwriter/dancer/painter, potter, etc.… create and innovate. We had large numbers of people who participated in classes, but the only place we could perform was at the high school auditorium which was huge … 1,400 seat house.

Doing published plays at that time and paying royalties, plus renting the theater, plus hiring sound and lighting people were out of our financial realm … so I would help kids write! I would come up with a theme and then encourage kids to bring whatever they had to auditions to create a role or place for them. That way we were doing something very different.

Using my skills as a writer and teaching them that skill as well as being ASSERTIVE.

Teach kids to constantly REINVENT themselves and do the WORK.

They would in a sense decide through those means which kids would shine for that show. We did it usually twice a year and sometimes three times a year with music, dance, acting, and a story that would weave everything together. We would also get adults in the community to interact with them, so there was something for everyone.

One time a young boy probably around 9, named Clay Helvie came in and sang the same song he did for the last show. I had to tell him there on the spot with our judges that he did it great for the previous play, but I couldn't use it again. Now, most people would crumble ... remember the story John Ratzenberger told me about pitching another idea ... that is what this 9-year old did. He loved Cher, so he sang a song from Cher, "Gypsy's Tramps and Thieves." He did a fine job and sounded like Cher. Again, we were stumped and told him we weren't sure how to incorporate that in the Christmas show. Most kids would have folded, but then Clay said ... what about "Christmas Shoes?"

We never heard it ... he sang it, and we were all in tears and made him the A-story of the show. The victory was that our students at a young age learned about being **ASSERTIVE** and being **RESILIENT.** Our kids did that all of the time.

To **REINVENT** themselves over and over again and to me, that was such a great life lesson. Every show was original, and every kid had a chance to shine.

Then a friend of mine named Dr. Keith Rockey, who was a Corporate Sponsor, believed in what we were doing and took it on his own to reach out to Penelope Knight, wife of the founder of Nike. Keith was good friends with her brother and was passionate to make a difference and a difference he made. The next thing that happened was a miracle, and I will let you read the letter I received from Mrs. Knight.

Dear Mark:

Enclosed please find my check in the amount of $150,000 as a contribution to the Community School of the Arts. I have increased the amount originally promised by $50,000 because I was so impressed by your recent email to Keith Rockey regarding this contribution. It is so refreshing to have an organization appreciate (rather than expect) a gift. If there is any public recognition, I would appreciate my donation mentioned in memory of my father, Alex L. Parks, who was a true lover of the arts and instilled this love in his five children.

I hope this donation might encourage others in your community to take note of such a fine program in their own neighborhood.

Very sincerely,

Penelope P. Knight
March 6, 2006

I was overwhelmed and flabbergasted. I was moved to tears that this could help so many kids. I created an endowment in her dad's name so kids in perpetuity would get scholarships under Alex L. Parks. I asked the kids to thank her who received scholarships and Dawn Darga created a fantastic presentation. I wrote Mrs. Knight a nice thank you letter from my heart, and she wrote me back with this.

Dear Mark:

I just received your packet of information from Keith Rockey this past weekend and I wanted to immediately write and thank you for such a nice presentation. I loved the notes from the students and parents, as well as the wonderful book detailing all of your works this past year. The program looks amazing! I was so pleased to see the money from the Alex Parks scholarship fund put to such good use.

I am enclosing with this letter an additional check in the amount of $100,000 to add to the established Alex L. Parks scholarship fund. I know you will disperse these scholarships to the most needy and talented children in the community, as in the past. I look forward to seeing the new projects which you develop this coming year.

Thank you for the opportunity to contribute to such a marvelous program. It is a pleasure to be involved with such a talented, artistic and hard-working community.

My best wishes for a successful year,

Penelope P. Knight

And then this ….

Mark:

The holiday season is upon us and I wanted to be among the first to wish you and the school a very Happy Holidays and best wishes for the coming New Year.

I have also enclosed a check in the amount of $100,000 to be added to the existing Alex L. Parks Scholarship Fund. I am very pleased with the work that you and the school have accomplished over the past several years. I enjoy the annual newsletter and photos which you send.

Thank you for the service you provide to the local community and the lives of the young people you serve.

Most sincerely,

Penelope P. Knight
December 12, 2011

What an angel Mrs. Knight was to us. CSA was now a recognizable brand! We had drawing, painting, cartooning, pottery, Zumba, yoga, acting, singing, writing, piano classes, violin, judo, Tai Kwon do, all kinds of dance and we were busting at the seams. We had one dance teacher making $150.00 an hour who came up from Indianapolis.

We hired over 50 people. Kids were coming to our school from out of town.

Talk about economic development ... we did it.

We started to fill up the Centrum mall with The Convention and Visitors Bureau, the Philharmonic, Main Street Marion and others.

Like anything in life ... with the good there is always bad, and greed came into play. Some teachers didn't like what other teachers made even though every teacher set their own price and their own curriculum. So those disgruntled teachers would up their price and then others would, and it was just gross, so we had to change the system to a scale system based on the number of kids they had.

Our wonderful owner of the building sold it to a gentleman who became greedy and wanted us to sign a two-year contract. We just couldn't do that yet because we didn't know what teachers were coming or going, and he gave us 30 days to leave. Man, I was livid at his greed! We always paid on time and brought so many other organizations into his building. Oh well ... the outcome was that we left, The Convention and Visitors Bureau, Main Street Marion and The Philharmonic all moved too, and the owner sold the empty building.

We worked with the City to get a huge empty downtown building. The deal was we had to pay 11 grand in back taxes, we needed 140 grand in the development of new classrooms, and we had two months to do it. I had a great friend and builder named Brad Pinkerton and his team who pulled off a miracle to get it done in time.

The building belonged to us, and we were responsible for all repairs. We discovered that the exterior brick was really interior brick and the integrity of the entire 4 story building was at stake. So, we wrote a grant and were blessed to get 265 thousand dollars.

$265 thousand was not enough to do all that we had to do ... so we had community champions paying for sponsorship panels of James Dean, Garfield, etc.... we had a brick campaign and friends from the community and my friends from St. Louis gave to the cause. James Dean's family and his cousin Marcus Winslow bought a stone and gave me a lot of James Dean memorabilia to put up throughout the school. We were so honored and did. Everyone gave. Massive volunteer hours by board members, volunteers, community people ... it was like *It's A Wonderful Life*.

If we needed a mechanical lift, Nick Wike would give us a lift for free. If we needed a limousine, Eddie Blinn would provide us with one for free.

If we needed the Splash House water park, the Parks Department would give it to us. If we needed to make rain for a commercial, the fire department would come out and simulate it. If we needed to close down traffic, the Police Department would help us. On two occasions we were desperate for a helicopter, and we called the Ott's, and they were there to help. We needed housing for an artist, and Greg Kitts put him up for a year for free. Comfort Suites would often give us free rooms for stars. Leonard Mathews was an IWU student who would bring an army of volunteers over to work on the building. If we needed commercials, Brighthouse and our Inge Harte would run them, or WBAT would have me on the radio, or The Chronicle-Tribune would do a great story. The local media deserves a lot of credit for telling the magical CSA story that became an economic development success story and even better than that a place where kids could dream and thrive.

Michael DeLuise spread his joy and magic with all of the kids on stage and in class.

I was passionate about teaching and helping kids … but a majority of my efforts went to raising money, so they could take classes with scholarships and building them a memorable place to play and create.

Some of our kids that earned their stripes would teach and make money by inspiring and educating younger kids. We had art for everybody and anybody. Remember Burt said **EVERYONE MATTERS!** So I started teaming up with Carey Services that had special needs students.

At first, it was just a class to become aware of the face, voice and body language to get them to understand things like sarcasm which was very hard for these loving friends of mine.

As time went on I felt they were ready to go on the big stage with everyone else and boy did they shine. They would always get the biggest ovation of every show, and I was beyond proud.

CSA were all my kids. Some came from troubled homes. Some were abused, some would confide in me that they couldn't read so I would protect them on all fronts. Some had trouble with eye contact so we would work on that. Some were deathly shy. It was my mission to not necessarily make them stars, but to just help them strive for excellence in whatever they did in the world and make a difference.

One thing that Burt taught me was to LOVE … let people know you love them and that was easy for me because I did and do. I would always tell the kids "Who loves you?" and they would respond … "You do"!

It was imperative for them to know I and many others loved them so dare to dream. Dare to fail, dare to take a risk and dare to reach for the stars and know no matter what you are loved.

Aubrey Miller from Disney came to teach a class and sign autographs.

We started bringing stars to town to act in our shows and teach our kids. My dear friend from Burt Reynolds, John D'Aquino was doing a hugely popular Disney Chanel show named *Cory In the House*. Michael DeLuise came with John, and they were greeted like rock stars! The community went nuts.

Kaleb is now like a son to me, but back then he just lost his dad. John D'Aquino came from LA to uplift him and other kids.

Kids learned from them and made CONNECTIONS. Adults and kids acted with them, and the self-esteem of the town grew. Our local talent started to realize they could hang with the best of the best and we were bringing Los Angeles and New York to Marion Indiana. Kaleb Evans was one of my students and had just lost his father, so we wrote a scene for John and Kaleb that instilled **FAITH** that someone special was always watching over him.

Rondell Sheridan came in for a camp.

Garreth Saxe from the *Lion King* taught a class.

David Hibbard from the Broadway show CATS here is acting with one of my star students KiLeigh Williams who is now in Los Angeles as a Professional dancer.

Local terrific actor Charles O'Haver with another star from LA Daniel Roebuck.

Sonya Tayeh came to teach dance and choreography, Ken Gorrell came and talked about Special Effects, Bill Bindley, my director from Madison, came to speak to the kids. My former apprentice classmate Merri Sugarman who is now a huge casting director in NY - taught a class and introduced her cast from the *Jersey Boys* to our kids. One never knew who would come to CSA and do what Burt did and pay it forward.

The Jersey Boys cast with our CSA kids.

A rare opportunity came where in addition to Michael DeLuise and John D'Aquino I could get Burt Reynolds to come to see how we paid his gift forward. If not for my friend John Boyle it would not have been possible. John was a huge sponsor and flew Burt in a private jet right to the Marion airport, and we treated him like gold.

The Marion Police Department's CERT team treated Burt like the Star he was, and in return, he treated them great and loved them. They watched over the Bandit 24/7.

Gigi Rice and Kim Chase are my dear friends.

Matt Harris, my cousin through marriage and neighbor, lent his Frank Lloyd Wright home so Burt could live in style. Two other apprentices of his and stars in their own right, came from LA to surprise him. Gigi Rice and Kim Chase.

Burt and I had a blast. I was so excited for him to see that we paid it forward with an art school in Marion Indiana named CSA.

I had my college roommates come up from St. Louis to play with us. The community packed the 1,400 hundred seat house and sold it out. **Marilu Henner** called in LIVE to surprise him.

Former apprentices like **Anastasia Barzee** from NY, **Lisa Soland** from Nashville, **Brent Sexton**, and Tommy Thompson from LA all former students on tape saying hi and paying tribute to our teacher.

As Burt was ready to leave the stage, the 1,400 patrons stood on their feet to honor my teacher, boss, mentor, and friend and it was so beautiful to see.

Mike Achor drove us around in a limo donated by Eddie Blinn and Greg Kitts. The Mill was packed to the rim. We stayed out very late and had a private table that John Boyle paid for the entire meal. The next morning, Cindy and **Courtney Gorman**, Cindy's mom, Debbie, and Doug Lance and of course **Dawn Darga** and **Julie Fauser** all made breakfast for Burt and our company.

Burt received a standing ovation from the 1,400 plus sold-out house in Marion Indiana.

With some of my best friends from Mizzou with the legendary Burt Reynolds. Roger Cagle, Jeff Brandt, Rick Survant, and Terry Engel and the MAN ... Burt Reynolds.

The famous "Burt Love Clutch" with one of my students KiLeigh Williams.

Scott Evans came up for a class and now is a big star for Access Hollywood.

Then it was sadly time for Burt to leave. A large police escort to the Marion Airport and like the STAR he was and always will be in my mind ... Burt went into the Jet courtesy of Mr. Boyle and headed back to Jupiter. He left a mark here. We created an endowment with his name on it **(https://givetogrant.org/csa-reynolds)** to help further kids at CSA who are serious about acting and taking it to the next level. This gift will only grow and will last in perpetuity to honor Burt and help kids.

Please look at the letter he wrote Julie and me. Enclosed was a check for a thousand dollars to put in his endowment to support more kids from Marion and Grant County.

Honoring Burt was my mission, and I was so happy he saw the lives he changed for teaching others to pay it forward. This is a pattern I hope my students keep doing and have faith they will.

Warner Brothers came to town to honor James Dean, and we did an original show to entertain them and the community. Many of the stars came to town and met our local talent.

Jason North was our first employed as an assistant to me, and he became James Dean. What an excellent job he and the cast did. Seen above with star Earl Holliman who knew Dean.

The Mayor hired me as the Director of Marketing for the City for nine years, and while there we continued to grow and grow at CSA. We had culinary classes, pottery, we had all forms of Martial Arts that came to us, and I needed another building. The Salin family donated a massive building to us a few doors down.

Whether it was winning dance competitions, having a monthly visual artist featured in our new art gallery, original shows, an annual art auction, a yearly go-kart race, dance shows, guest artist series, there was always something new and exciting at CSA. Four of my board members Dawn Darga, Lori Eltzroth, Carol Hamilton, and Carla Tucker won the prestigious Athena Award for their service to CSA. Then I was blessed to receive the Governor's Arts Award from Governor Mitch Daniels.

Governor Mitch Daniels gave me the prestigious Indiana Governors Arts Award in which I paid tribute to Burt Reynolds.

My good friends Scott and Julie Moorehead overwhelmed me with a substantial annual $125,000.00 a year gift for scholarships so more kids could enjoy the arts. WOW!!! That was a game changer! Boy, do I love them for seeing what we did and making such a giant difference!

My kids and community were leaping for joy! The best of people came out and helped build something amazing Because of Burt.

If you had a dream with a plan, we would do what we could to get it done. My friend Kory Browder wanted to direct *The Nutcracker* with the Philharmonic and make it an annual tradition … so we did, and she did a fantastic job. I usually would stay out of acting, but she wanted me in it, and I had a blast. I incorporated my special needs students with their magic to help me make the Nutcracker come to life.

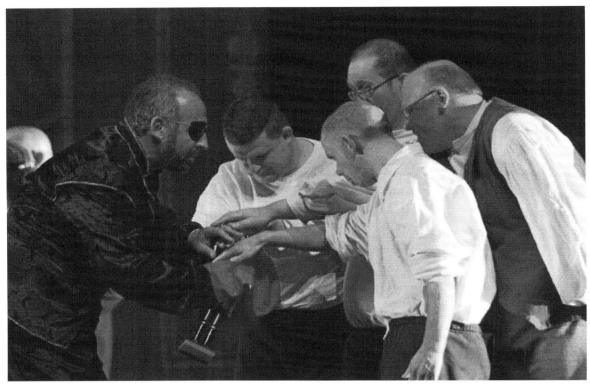
My Special Needs students had the magic touch to make the Nutcracker come to life and inspire our community.

Like Vince McMahon in the WWE, I lived and breathed CSA. It was 24/7 all year long combined with being the Director of Marketing for the City for nine years. I was always working. I would go on vacations with my family and think of the kids I still had to write for and stress over kids I couldn't serve better. I wouldn't sleep because they needed me, and they were my kids. Three CSA kids ran away from home and came to CSA because it was there where they felt safe. They shared with us that their father was sexually molesting them. Social services and the police worked with me to help the kids be safe, and the parent was put in jail.

I truly loved serving CSA with every fiber in my being. I pushed the staff hard to greet everyone with a smile. To go the extra mile to love, be excellent and make CSA a beacon of hope and light to the Community. There was great joy in making a difference, but constant stress and I was getting further and further away from my own art.

I was writing movies whenever I could on the side. In 2013, I wrote a movie called *Standby* which I was going to direct and had Burt Reynolds, Jason Alexander, Bruce Dern, Gigi Rice, Emanuelle Chriqui attached and had most of the money and was trying to get Michael Keaton as the lead. This was before *Birdman* … but the money fell short. For me, that would have been what the doctor ordered because it would have allowed me to still do MY art, bring more attention to our school and our kids because nobody could go at that pace forever. One thing I blame myself only for and nobody else is that I didn't honor my own art. I gave time, talent and treasure to a cause that I loved and believed in. However, I worked so hard to become a professional artist and while at CSA everything artistically I did was for free. Everything. It was my choice … again … I take full responsibility for it … and did what I had to do to build the school. However, since I devalued my own art and time, why shouldn't others devalue my art and time?

I was asked to open the school for kids on Sunday and help kids for free with auditions on Friday night and leave my own family functions. I was expected to act and write for free over and over again. We would value the dancer who came in from out of town or the professional actor, and I would have to find the money to pay them. At the same time, I was just giving my art away for free, and after 12 years it no longer felt right, and I had nothing else to give. At one time, the board asked me if I wanted CSA as my own business. Of course, I said no because I was there to serve the community and I was so glad I did. What an honor and joy it was to do so.

LETTERS

An amazing town

Editor's note: the below letter was penned by Burt Reynolds, who passed away Thursday, Sept. 6. Reynolds wrote the letter to Mark and Julie Fauser soon after visiting Marion.

Mark and Julie,

I want both of you to know how wonderful you made me feel this past weekend. It's an amazing town with beautiful people inside and out. There is no hidden agenda inside anyone. The sweetness and kindness is so real it's too good to be true. But it's all sincere – full of truth, genuinely deep, from the bottom of everyone's heart!

I feel so privileged to be a part of such a lyrical, romantic, and unique small town. I hope I can come back – but first you owe me a visit. I have room for the whole family.

Have a wonderful and happy new year.

My love always,
Burt

With two 18 thousand square foot buildings debt-free. $125,000,00 in scholarships annually by my friends the Mooreheads. The angel Penelope Knight and the Alex L Parks endowment. Then we created one for James Dean and Jim Davis. We had an Art Gallery, the endowment for Burt Reynolds and we had virtually every kind of art you could dream of and massive community support.

We did what we needed to do. We created jobs and life to the downtown. Now it is an accredited art school, and we paid it forward Because of Burt Reynolds …

... CSA STUDENTS PAY IT FORWARD

With two of my many awesome students. Caleb "The Fitness Marshall" Marshall and Regan Reese

Caleb, "The Fitness Marshall," is a YouTube sensation helping millions of people with his entertaining, and imaginative exercise routines which he started teaching at CSA. As a young boy and throughout he was one of my star students who could sing, act, dance, direct, edit and create and now he is paying it forward. We have many kids working professionally as artists, and I am so proud of them, but I am equally impressed of my kids that became passionate/excellent Doctors, Marketing Directors, Teachers, Military service, Special needs instructors, firemen, mothers, etc....

I love all my CSA kids and couldn't be prouder of them and look forward to what positive things they do in the world to make a difference and pay it forward Because of Burt ...

... MAKING A MARK

Making a Mark was a documentary produced about me/Burt through Taylor University. It was all about paying it forward, and Burt is in the documentary along with John D'Aquino. I was so humbled that they did that. When I was in Florida Burt, and his class watched it. It was so nice to honor him again and see his gifts come full circle. I continue to write and am blessed to work as the Sales, Marketing and Creative Development Director of Marion Community Schools. We have a great Superintendent, and our enrollment is up for the first time since the '70s. The kids are wonderful, and it's an honor to make a difference there.

I wrote a movie with my friend Charles O'Haver very loosely based on our small town's annual Easter Pageant ... the logline is that the small city is so passionate about putting on their Easter Pageant that they break the ten commandments to do it. We wrote the lead for Burt, and he wanted to do it and what a great way to give back to him, but sadly now that will never happen with him. I continue to write and am finishing up a musical about James Dean seen through the eyes of his Guardian Angel called Cool's Angel ...

My greatest creation, however, is by far my family. I met my wife at Burt's school, and we now have 3 beautiful kids that Burt has been a part of their growth and again .... This blessing in my mind is Because of Burt ...

... FAMILY

My greatest creation was my family. Nothing I could ever produce would be better than the kids that my wife and I are so lucky to have. Let's be clear Because of Burt I met my wife, who is a great mother. Burt took great pride in my kids, and we all owe Burt a debt of gratitude. Whether we were on the set with him, in his class or home. He threw a baby shower for my wife and daughter to be.

Burt on stage shaking Jack's hand with Julie behind Jack, and Kiki and Nick also ready to greet the man they grew up with.

When I didn't think Burt knew my name at his school, my mom thought it was because I looked like I cared too much in the picture with him. Look at my mom with Burt. It's hard not to look excited when you are next to Burt – huh mom? LOL

All of my kids were at CSA, and now my oldest son Nick is in the Airforce, Kiki is a Marketing guru for a large law firm, and my youngest Jack is an All NCC Tennis Star in High School.

Burt gave me this tremendous blessing, but as I stated earlier, I am just one of many Because of Burt Stories …

... FINAL CURTAIN

I met Adam Rifkin in Burt's class when he said "I will only do the movie *The Last Movie Star* if Burt Reynolds starred in it" and then they made it. I knew Burt wanted to come back to Marion and I wanted him back. I wanted to give more back to him artistically. There was so much more to do so the world could see his underrated talent and generous heart.

My Brit class 30th reunion with Burt

It was September and Burt was so excited to do the movie with Quentin Tarantino and the All-Star cast in October. While working on his lines Burt's loving, giving heart of 82 years gave out, and he passed away. It's hard for me to fathom that the guy who was so tough ... the guy who did his own stunts rolling out of a car, catching on fire, or broke his hand right in front of me was gone.

The megastar who soared and crashed but like a Phoenix would rise again and again would never rise again. At least not in the physical sense.

Ironically, Burt's funeral was on September 19th, 2018 which was my birthday. How fitting and what a connection between us. I have **FAITH** that there is more to come Because of Burt ...

A cartoon was drawn by my friend Jack Marshall of Burt, John D'Aquino, myself and Michael DeLuise.

Apprentices from different eras at Burt's funeral!

Me at his Gate after the funeral!

... CURTAIN CALL

Burt is one of the most iconic movie stars in cinematic history. Period. He won Golden Globes, Emmy's and tons of People Choice Awards. He will go down as one of the all-time best. Burt Reynolds heart that eventually failed his physical body was his greatest asset. He fought for Sally Field when others wouldn't, and although she always had the talent, he used his clout to put her on a beautiful well-deserved wave.

Remember talent is not everything it is CONNECTIONS and TIMING and she had a huge player in her corner. If it's of any comfort to Sally, he talked to me often about her and took responsibility for his mistakes and had nothing but great things to say about her. Farrah Fawcett was also denied support from the Studio to do "Cannonball Run" so Burt gave her part of his salary and then her career took off. Burt believed in people more than they believed in themselves and if you were smart to seize the opportunity when he opened the door good things would come.

As stated, I am one of many Because of Burt stories ... there are countless other success stories courtesy of Burt Reynolds. I hope this book sheds light on what a great person Burt Reynolds was and inspires the reader to make a Mark in life and Pay it Forward.

Jupiter Florida was at one time a small town, but Burt was so proud of it. He bragged about it on the Tonight Show. He sunk in his own time, talent and treasure into that city and now it is a wealthy community that Tiger Woods, and so many other successful people live.

One of my dreams is that the Maltz Theater ... that Burt originally built ... and one of his former waiters, Andrew Kato (now the Executive Director) receives the money to complete its add-on to help more students and artists in Burt's name. My hope is that the add on is named after Burt Reynolds.

Burt for many years did not want to step foot back into that place because of the hurt of losing something so special to him. In the last few years he told me factually he would be honored to have his name back on that building that would stand the test of time that benefits artists. The students he worked with in Mall Space to Mall Space would have that as their permanent home too, and everyone would come together to honor Mr. Reynolds. So please Jupiter, West Palm Beach, Florida, Stars, friends, and readers of this book help me pay it forward and let's honor Burt Reynolds in a big collective way.

In Fairmount Indiana they have thousands of people come every year to honor James Dean, who only did three movies. When I come down to Jupiter every March ... I want to see Burt Reynolds everywhere. I want the world to know of his giving heart and for us to do the right thing and honor the man who gave so much to so many and we should do it Because of Burt...

God Bless you, Burt Reynolds … I will honor you forever!   Mark Fauser

The End

Made in the USA
Middletown, DE
13 April 2019